Where The Water Lilies Grow

Where the
Water Lilies Grow

R.D. Lawrence

Natural Heritage Books

Where The Water Lilies Grow
R.D. Lawrence

Published by Natural Heritage / Natural History Inc.
P.O. Box 95, Station O, Toronto, Ontario M4A 2M8

Summer 1999

Canadian Cataloguing in Publication Data

Lawrence, R.D. (Ronald Douglas), 1921 -
  Where the water lilies grow
Includes index.
ISBN 1-896219-52-7
1. Zoology — Ontario. 2. Animal behavior — Ontario. I. Title.
QL751.L3 1999   591.9713   C99-930513-1

Design by Steve Eby Production & Design

Printed and bound in Canada by Hignell Printing Ltd.,
Winnipeg, Manitoba.

THE CANADA COUNCIL | LE CONSEIL DES ARTS
FOR THE ARTS | DU CANADA
SINCE 1957 | DEPUIS 1957

Natural Heritage / Natural History Inc. acknowledges the support received for its publishing program from the Canada Council Block Grant Program. We also acknowledge with gratitude the assistance of the Association for the Export of Canadian Books, Ottawa.

Introduction

THIS BOOK, a sequel to "The Place in the Forest," tells of the wildlife around a lake near the author's home in the backwoods of Canada.

The author, with a knowledge born of much patient watching and waiting, tells the story of the animals who inhabit the lakeside, from the smallest water creature to the wolves, deer, and innumerable birds. His sensitivity, enthusiasm and empathy with the wildlife, and his detailed understanding of their habits, makes this a book that will engross even those who rarely venture beyond their urban environs.

Authoritatively written and beautifully illustrated with many of the author's own photographs, Lawrence's words conjure up the sounds, the smells and the very feel of the lakeside life in every season, a spectrum of life so intricate as to be almost beyond the limit of human understanding.

Table of Contents

Illustrations

ONE

A DRIVEN SLEET-RAIN pelted the surface of the lake, pockmarking it with its virulence. Brown riffles stirred the wind as icy droplets collided with the water, hitting down into it, breaking it and creating more, smaller droplets that fanned upwards in reversed cones, momentarily clung to their form and were then swallowed by the storm and their parent's body. Processions of dying leaves gyrated through the air, wobbling, skimming, dancing; forms of many hues, of diverse contours; some curled and warped, others freshly plucked from their branches, seemingly eager for this last adventure. Russet and scarlet and brown and yellow and silver; the pigments of autumn bedaubing the canvas of creation with surrealistic artistry unequalled.

Autumn on the lake, the dying time. Pathos, sweetness, poetry; a potpourri of feelings invoked in the human breast. Danger, escape, sleep; the admixture of instincts born into the creatures and plants of a northern wilderness. Today the pelting, ice-filled rain, tomorrow the white of snow. Yesterday the shrill honking of wild geese high above, now the drumming of rain on furrowed water, the squelch of wet upon the land. This is my wilderness and as I stand here, wet and cold and content, I see more than just a rain-soaked landscape upon which a small, rocky lake has been slashed; I see a thousand things, and they are all intimate. I see the bubbles bursting upon the surface of the lake as an invisible beaver swims towards his lodge; I see the leaves of the maple scurry by, scarlet flashes against the grey of cloud. I see the bulrushes shaken by more than the wind, for there are ducks still here and they shelter amongst the brown stems with the fluffy, down-filled tops. At my feet a set of tracks, small ones, perhaps two inches long but scarcely that wide and my eyes tell me that a red fox has stepped here not long ago, for the imprint of his claws and his pads are still clear and unbroken by the rain. Over there, upon a granite uplift, a few shreds of pine cone cling, the remnants of a squirrel's husbanding. Beside me a small aspen, a young tree, perhaps only seven seasons old; in its slender crotch the carefully woven nest of a warbler, a home used and now abandoned as its builder fans southward for warmth and safety. The sights of this day are endless, pleasant, fulfilling.

My wilderness…but is it my wilderness? Can any man lay claim to any part of this planet earth? Does not the earth, rather, claim man? By legal tenets in this century and society I own this piece of wild land, yet it can never be truly mine and it will exist long, long after my own body has been assimilated into earthmaking matter. Some other man may one day 'own' it, and yet, it will outlive him, too. How many other men have considered this their land, I wonder? Who and what were they? The first, no doubt, were dusky men, primitives we call them now, who claimed this soil and its waters by right of tenure and arms. Then came others, less dark, more capable, with better weapons and they took this land from the primitives. And so it has gone, and so it will undoubtedly continue to go, and no man will own my wilderness and all men will instead be owned by it.

These are some of the thoughts of autumn that claim me as I stand in the rain. They have been bred by this land which I have now known for twenty seasons. If sometimes they are but flashes of strange reason, they lead me inexorably into the contemplation of this forest and this lake and of those things that are in it and under it and above it. The trees and the birds; the fish and the insects and the animals and the rocks and the earth and the water. And I must tell of them, they impel me to this. And if my narration be good it is because of them; and if the telling is bad, it is because of me, because I have failed to understand, to feel for the things of the forest.

Autumn is a fitting time to begin my description of this place where the water lilies grow. A growing year has been born and has roistered and matured and fulfilled itself and is now ageing. Dying with dignity, its requiem is the song of the wind and the patter of the rain, the flight of the birds, their dwindling calls faint, high notes of farewell that contain a promise of return.

Yesterday I was here also and there was no rain. I heard the geese and raised my eyes to them and one laggard flew low, as though taking one last look at this place where it was born. With his gimlet eyes he must have noted the shape of his birthplace, a long, lean body of murky water studded by small rock islands; a lake that measures a mile-and-a-half in length and barely one quarter of a mile in width. It is broad in its southern beam; dart-narrow at its northern apex; pinched at its middle, as though east tried here to meet west and pushed earth and rocks into the water.

Around this lake are the trees, many species of them, hardwoods and softwoods; evergreen and deciduous growths. White pines, old and stately, gently waving their spread arms; aspens, whitish, dusty bark gleaming, branches almost denuded; maples, tall and branchy, mostly naked but stubbornly clinging to a few flaming leaves; oaks, gnarled veterans standing mostly alone, stubborn warriors surrounded by strangers; balsam firs, green cones that offer shelter to many things; spruces, sharp-needled trees of scaly bark. Here and there a stunted cedar clings precariously to rocky soil.

Around the trees are the bushes; the alders and willows and hazels and the sumac. And around these, the smaller plants; the blueberries and the brambles and the dwarf junipers, themselves jostled by the ferns. Below all this are the grasses; the wild strawberries, the mosses, the lichens, all the lesser plants of the wild which are yet greater than the remaining earthlife, the minute fungi, and tiny sproutlings that must face the danger of winter before they can hope to gain stature.

These things of green life, the great ones and the humble ones, combine with the lake and its water to create a fertile valley in which dwells a multitude of creatures. Each species in its own way provides something to the whole; some only a little, others a large helping, but there is one substance without which none of the others can live, which is of such magnitude to the life of our entire planet that without it our world would crumble. This element of magic is water, a simple liquid; one which, as every schoolboy knows, contains two atoms of hydrogen for every atom of oxygen. Simple and vital, that is water. Some two-thirds of the total body weight of all mammals is made up of it. Our very bones contain about 20 per cent of water; our brains contain 85 per cent of it. Within the bodies of mammals, birds, fish, reptiles, amphibians, insects and plants many chemicals exist and supply life. Some of these are complex, of great importance to the living, yet all would be helpless without water. Water dissolves them so that they may travel through their host-body; water gives them a medium in which to react, to combine (in some cases) with another and thus form another more complex chemical or provide food for their host. Water also helps to remove from the body its waste produces; it enters the kidneys and cleans them and carries away impurities through the urine channels; it enters the bowels and helps lubricate them and, by mixing with the solid wastes, eases their passage to the outside. Water in pure form absorbs heat and protects the body from sudden changes in temperature; by changing itself from liquid to gas, water can absorb even more heat and thus cools the body by the process of evaporation when the host perspires.

Because it can absorb heat, it also follows that it can carry heat and this is another vital function, for, by circulating in the blood through the body, water evenly distributes heat through the tissues. And, as a last service of life, water provides a lubrication for the body. Wherever one living organ rubs against another one, there you will find water, furnishing a cushion, lubricating permanently a sinew, a muscle, or a joint.

My wilderness lake never ceases to remind me of the value of the liquid which fills it and I find it even more marvellous to consider that every drop of this rather turgid water has found its way here from one of the oceans of the world, for these great seas of ours are the world's reservoirs. Harnessing the aid of the sun, the salt-filled sea water vaporizes, loses its salt and rises into the heavens to form clouds. Then the winds shepherd them, push them over the land. Now these vapour clouds cool and the gaseous moisture within them becomes heavy and drops to earth, to soak into the land, to follow rivers and streams, to drop into my lake. In time, each and every droplet that has fallen into this small lake will return to one of our seas. It may go there directly, reversing the process of evaporation with which it began its journey, or it may travel to its ancestral home in the body of one animal, or bird, or insect; or it may travel through the bodies of many animals before it ends its journey, for its ways are many and wonderful.

So, too, are the ways of my lake. It is small, as lakes go, and a little ragged in appearance. It is not a deep lake, and its water is brown, yet from rocky bank to swampy shoreline it is crammed with interest and beauty and secrets and life and death. There are many lakes like this one in many lands and mostly they go unnoticed, for man delights in the grand and tends to ignore the humble. I did, once. I have learned better since then. Now I scan every new living thing that my eyes fall upon and the familiar, too, comes in for close scrutiny and in this way I discover a little of the world of wilderness, the real world, which is quiet and humble and secretive. This real world demands affection and great patience from the human who would learn of the multitude of things that lurk almost unnoticed within it.

Though I have known my lake intimately for five years, it is still a near-stranger to me and, if this is a seeming-contradiction, a little patience will elicit an explanation. I came here first one late afternoon in autumn, my wife Joan beside me, our eyes seeing nothing but the green, shapeless form of a forest. We followed a path, little more than a track, and cleared timber to find ourselves before this lake. Its glory, the waxen blooms of yellow and white lilies, was passed; its waters, browned by algae and the debris of the lake life, were uninviting; its shores either granite forms of grey or reedy morasses of mud and beaver leavings. An ordinary, ugly little lake, sculpted ages ago by upheavals that split the earth's surface.

Its story begins, I suppose, about one-and-a-half billion years ago (more or less!) during a time which geologists now call the Proterozoic period. Then the earth was sheathed in sedimentation and subjected to enormous volcanic explosions; and to erosion, and to great ice masses, which retreated, leaving in their wake more sediments. Then they came again, to pound and scrape, pressing frozen, marching irresistibly, and slowly retreating northwards anew. One billion years passed thus and during this infinity life formed; primitive life, finding substance in the ice waters that were trapped in holes and depressions all over the planet. Came the algae, the fungi. Then were born minute bits of life in the seas called protozoa and these were followed by shellfish and worms.

With the passing of the Proterozoic age, a new, mild time came and the sluggish life that existed took hold and multiplied itself and began to change. This was the advent of the Cambrian period, which, man now believes, began 585 million years ago and lasted for 80 million years. Now there were low lands, and early rocks formed. More algae; more life: primitive trilobites and brachiapods and the ancestors of today's creatures became established.

So it went, slowness and growth and great spans of time, and one geologic Period slipped by and was replaced by another: Ordovician, Silurian, Devonian, Mississippian, Pennsylvanian, Permian, Triassic, Jurassic, Cretaceous. Now the Rocky Mountains raised their spires in western North America, 135 million years ago. And my lake was doubtlessly already old by human standards and there was life in it: dinosaurs, toothed birds, the beginnings of the first 'modern' birds; the progenitors of today's mammals. Then more time and more periods. This was the age of mammals and the birth of important times on earth, now labelled Epochs to distinguish them from the Periods because of the longer duration of the latter and the relatively rapid developments which took place during the former. The Tertiary Period began 75 million years ago and brought with it the Epochs: Paleocene, Eocene, Oligocene, Miocene and Piliocene, which saw man rise upright after he climbed down from the trees.

Next came the Quaternary Period which ushered two more Epochs, Pleistocene and Recent. The former came one million years ago and lasted a like time. It brought disasters to life and sheathed my lake with cold during four separate ages of ice. It exterminated many species, changed others, saw the beginnings of social habit amongst the men of the day. Then it ended and 'modern' affairs began to shape themselves on and around and inside my lake some 250,000 years ago. The last ice retreated and the sun once again warmed the land; some ancient plants died and new ones replaced them. This was the true age of man; it marked the beginning of the destruction by him of many precious things; it brought wealth to the mind and saw all things subjected to the will of humanity.

This is the biographic sketch of my lake. It has taken a short time to write, yet it covers a span of time too immense to visualize. It charts an infinitely brief course through the happenings, the countless, patient happenings, that evolved here. They challenge the mind, defying it ever to discover more than just the minutest fraction of all that has transpired during one-and-a-half billion years. How, then, can this body of water, these trees and plants and rocks and creatures of life, be other than strangers to me after an acquaintance that has lasted but a mere five years?

Today is Sunday, tonight I leave my lake for another five days of city dwelling. I am loath to turn from this spot, despite the rain, for I have not yet seen enough. So I linger awhile, listening to the drumming of the rain, to the hoarseness of a bullfrog who is undoubtedly thinking of the long sleep that lies ahead. A blue jay flits from hazel to pine to poplar and eyes me critically before it launches itself away from man, its shrill, harsh call a scolding. This is one of this year's brood, judging from the dark cheek patches and the untidy head, a late comer preparing already for winter, and he makes me think of the grey jays, who are not yet here but whom I expect daily if they have survived their migration to the northland. For three years they have come; attending our doings with interest that is sharpened by their hunger, for they are rogues of great appetite, these fluffy, inquisitive birds, and they have little fear of man. The first year came two birds and these stayed through the winter and had their young in February, during the time of deep snow, and big cold and five grey shapes flew away in early June. Four birds returned the next autumn and eight left in May. Six came back. A hunting hawk killed one of these and I watched its death. Another one disappeared and four were left and they bred and there were again nine grey jays in the trees beside my lake. How many will return this year I wonder?

A pileated woodpecker male flaps wetly overhead, his black and white wings shishing above the sounds of the wind and the rain. I watch him disappear in a tangle of trees at the far, northern end of the lake. I turn away at last, but I avoid the trail that leads to the highway and instead squeeze myself between the brush and trees of the wet forest. A quarter of a mile west of the lake is my cabin. Joan is there, probably worrying over our raccoons, for we have seven of them now and she frets for them when the summer goes and the autumn brings the cold. Yet they always find shelter and spring brings them to us again, a little lean, made timid by their long rest, tired after their mating fights, but still retaining their trust in us and eager for the titbits: the cake and the marsh-mallows and the peanuts and the meats.

THE WILDERNESS is a strange mistress. She is gentle, fierce, tender, strong, pitiless and compassionate; above all she is capricious and it follows that she is also dangerous. Her creatures know this with that deep instinct that is born in all things that are wild and free; but man must learn it slowly, often painfully, and sometimes never at all. The wilderness can bewitch. Some men need but a gentle touch and they become enslaved to her, perhaps unknowing, at times rebelliously, often willingly and passionately.

The wilderness is ageless and ancient, deathless and full of death; lifeless and full of life. The wilderness is contradiction and logic; it is an endless procession of events which, when seen, fill with wonder their viewer...

Some years ago now, I first met the wilderness of North America. I blundered into it in mid-winter, an ignorant immigrant unknowing of its ways, my very ignorance a challenge. For more than 1,000 miles I travelled through it, courting death daily yet not realizing my risks. I will ill-equipped, for I had asked no one about the places to which I planned to travel. I was green, a tenderfoot on the loose in a land he should have avoided. That I survived I owe to the wilderness, not to my own efforts, for after the first 100 miles good sense should have penetrated through my pate. It did not, and I persisted northward through country in which for days I was the only human and which was gripped by ice and snow and temperatures of minus 30 and 40 degrees.

Strangely, I had no reason for going. The journey was as illogical a one as could be. It just came to me one day in December that I had left Europe and had come to this continent and the only thing that the move had achieved for me was a change of cities. In Britain I had read of the Northland. I had seen photographs of it and Hollywood epics made in it. Suddenly I felt I must go and see for myself and I left, driving an ageing car, my only precautionary equipment a small hand axe, a hastily-purchased parka and a pair of ankle boots. For the rest of me, I was clad for winter in the city.

Even more strange, though, is that after I had made my journey, after I had lived in the wilderness two-and-a-half years, I left it with little conscious knowledge of it. In those days the affair had simply been an experience, like visiting Niagara Falls, or some such landmark of tourist interest. And yet the wilderness had put its mark on me. I pursued my affairs for two or three years, outwardly unchanged, inwardly seized by a strange, new restlessness which I did not then understand. At times I returned to the fringes of the wild for short periods, did some fishing, or hunting, enjoyed the outings and was content to return to the orderly humdrum of a life civilized. Yet the wilderness was working within me.

One day I boarded a plane and headed north on a routine feature story. Churchill, on the Hudson's Bay, was my destination, a place hardly Arctic by northern standards. I found lodging in one

of its two hotels, set out for my interviews and pictures and returned to my room six hours later. It was late evening and, as I prepared to open my portable typewriter, the husky dogs of the Inuit started their nightly serenade. Their noise was almost wolfish, but not quite; yet it set loose a reaction in me. Suddenly I realized that I had missed the howling of the timber wolves; the peeping of the grouse; the rustle of the trees during the dark of night.

Memory of the wilderness came to me and now it held meaning. Knowledge must have been stored somewhere in my subconscious, for things that I had not noticed during my sojourn in the wilds now began to crowd my memory: intriguing, interesting, impelling me to new journeys, which I made. But now my eyes were open and my knowledge was put to use and slowly a new world unfolded before me.

Then one day I found my lake and the land upon which I was to build a cabin. It was then the dormant power of the wilderness exerted itself and I devoted myself to the study of things wild. And in this way I found what I suppose every man seeks, true freedom, and though this was not yet a permanent state for me, still those spells of it were enough to sustain me while I engaged in affairs of civilized living. But now, while enclosed in a city, there was the knowledge that the wilderness and its freedom waited. My restlessness left and my mind became clearer and patience, a quality which I had scarcely enjoyed until then, entered into my scheme of things, weak yet, for I was born an impatient being, but steadily gaining strength and influence.

At first I studied the environments of my cabin, a quarter of a mile from the lake, specializing in these, as it were, and saving the lake for another time, though never really able to keep away from it altogether. I have described my land and its creatures and plants elsewhere, but while centering my attentions on the place of the water lilies, still many of my cabin-creatures, as I think of them, have a place in this narrative, for they, too, visit the lake and are a part of it.

As I SAT on a rock one morning during a sun-filled autumn day, I looked intently at the small lake, glistening and moving before me and I asked myself: what is a lake? My answer was immediate but vague: an ecosystem. Of course this was not good enough. Scientifically explained, the term is used to define 'a natural unit of living and non-living things which act, one upon the other, to produce a more or less stable state, or system, in which the exchange of materials between the living and the non-living pursues a circular route.' Now, the lay reader may be forgiven if this last sentence confuses him. I give it here merely to draw attention to a rather dry, unpoetic scientific description.

When the term came to my mind I understood it, yet its full meaning was clouded, until I began to fit the pieces together. Then, bit by bit, there emerged a clear answer. To understand an ecosystem it is first necessary to understand the 'circle of life,' which, starting with the sun as a source of energy, develops plant life which is eaten by small animal life, which is in turn eaten by larger animal life. The remains of these killings (and the remains of plants and creatures that die of old age or disease), bits not eaten, body juices, bone, and fur, and scales, become dead matter that are food for creatures known as decomposer organisms—fungi and bacteria—which convert these wastes into substances usable by green plants to form life anew. These substances have been given many names: the farmer calls them manure, or fertilizer; to the gardener they are humus; and the scientist refers to them as inorganic matter, that is, matter that is capable of giving or sustaining life yet which does not itself possess body organs, without which no true life can exist. This is the circle of life, preordained, a stable mixture of the living and the dead, one dependent upon the other. This is also an ecosystem.

Probing with the aid of a microscope focused on a drop of lake water, it is possible to see a number of intricately-made objects jostling each other in their minute liquid world. Collectively these insignificant bits are called plankton (from the Greek πλγγκτον,

The Lake, a support for many forms of life.

meaning wandering and now referring to a moving mass of animal or vegetable bodies too small to be seen individually by the naked eye, but noticeable when they are congregated in numbers). These creatures are the primary supply of life in a world of water. They are divided into two general classifications: zooplankton (animal life) and phytoplankon (vegetable life). Alone each invisible fleck is nothing, as a group they are a vital part of the circle of life; take them away and you break the circle; break the circle and there will be vacuum, nothing.

It takes time and some practice to recognize all these tiny things frolicking within a drop of water. Which is which? Is that one a zooplankton or a phytoplankton? Let us see... There is one, it looks like a minute set of horns taken from the head of one of those famed Texan steers. Beside it is another, a round fluffy-look-ing ball with a little stalk at one end; and yet another, this one shaped like a crescent moon and near it a tiny snake-like thing composed of even tinier circles, chain-like. So they go, many dif-ferent bits of vegetable plankton, the producer organisms of the waters. Now another life speck is visible. Is it a flea? It looks like one, certainly, but it is far too small, and its legs are feathery, its tail pointy, so is its 'nose' and its body seems criss-crossed with lines. Watching it, the eye notes its actions. It has darted at one of those little crescent moons and has gulped it down. Now another crea-ture comes into focus. This one is even stranger. It looks like a rather squat torpedo, complete with steering fins at its thin end. It has bands wrapped about itself, evenly spaced; it has a mass of 'hair' growing from its right side and twin tentacles, hairy, ending in a sparse bunch of thin feelers. These are animal plankton and there are others similar to them and they are the primary con-sumers of the lake, the vegetable eaters.

Waiting for these last creatures, back there in the lake, are the secondary consumers, the small meat eaters, visible these; beetles and their larva and new-hatched fish. And they are chased, caught and devoured by the tertiary consumers, the bigger fish. And root-ed around the lake are the bigger plants, also producers, for they, too, are food for others; and in the lake, deeper, are wormy things and little dot things and chain things, invisible without the microscope. These are the reducer organisms, the decomposers, the fungi and the bacteria. And still deeper in the water, and in the bottom of the lake, are inorganic compounds mixed with minute organic beings. And, crawling along the bottom, are bigger, visible worms and larvae, who are also primary consumers of vegetable until they, too, become food for one of the lake's carnivores.

These are the creatures of the lake. They must live here until death takes them, to hold them for a time until their bodies give life to other things. They are the true inhabitants of the lake, specialists that keep the water sweet and provide food for the land things that come to the lake, and for the things of the air. And some of these creatures of land and of air are so dependent upon the lake and its waters and its contents that they cannot live without it. Some come here only occasionally; yet others live beside it. But all things need the water of the lake, the fluid of birth which spawned the world and all that is upon it.

TWO

DAWN. AND SILENCE; and the sluggish white mists upon the water, low-lying and tattered in places, wraiths hiding the glassy surface of the lake. Frost glistens in the pale rose of a sun not yet risen; young frost, with just a touch of bite, which settled last night on grass and on small wet places. It paved thinly the trails of the beaver; it coated the webs of spiders; it stiffened the fallen leaves; it made brittle the morning.

Sunrise. The leading edge of the sun's fire bursts over the distant evergreens. The wilderness flashes; the mists recoil; the young frost dies. Still the light has not yet come full. The shadows are long, the day is a division of yellow and dark. Silence lingers a moment more and then is put to flight. Soft lapping by the water's edge midway up the lake—on the west shore, where the ancient rock is smoothed into a gradual, granite beach—intrudes fully upon the day.

Now the hoarse scream of a jay. It is answered by the cry of a woodpecker. Somewhere upon the water a beaver splashes. Chickadees whistle and a red squirrel chatters nervously as it watches those that are drinking.

Morning. The fullness of day where moments before night still lingered. Morning, suddenly, startlingly, the ritual change so old, yet still so breathtaking. On the granite rock the drinkers pause and raise furred heads to the sunlight, eyes lidded against the new glare. It is time to go, to seek a bed in some thicket and sleep until the sky again dims, for this is the way of the wolf. Briefly a scene. Five grey-fawn shapes silhouetted against the sunlight, backdropped by the browns and greens of the forest. Two stand on all fours, heads turns to the east, nostrils snuffling a newly-risen breeze. Two sit on their haunches, mouths slightly agape, tongues hanging free and dripping moisture; one is crouched, haunches

upright, shoulders bowed, front legs spread, head held high. The pack is still for a fraction of time, bellies sated, thirst quenched, muscles relaxed, legs stilled a pace away from movements; the young wolves—the two sitting, the one crouching—bubbling enthusiasm, desire for a last frolic agleam in their eyes. The parents habitual, careful, sensitive to the mood of the forest; eyes and ears and noses attuned to the day. Abruptly the scene ends. Lithe bodies turn from the water and the pack is gone, the dog leading, the bitch a shoulder behind him, the three young wolves fanned at their heels. The wilderness swallows them.

Time is nothing during this morning in late October. A clock's persistent, boring tick would be an insult to this day. The wolves have gone and the sun is a little higher and more birds sing and the last of the mists swirl upwards. And now the deer trot gracefully out of the trees. Comes an old doe, her twins, their birthspots but faint disturbances on their red hides, following; they are too old to nurse, but they still try to grasp their mother's withered dugs. Two yearlings now, dainty, blushing with the deep hues of autumnal condition, leap in unison over a fallen tree. The small black hoofs make hardly a sound, the long, slender legs whisk through the underbrush with inborn stealth.

Where the wolves drank, the deer stoop to wet the velvet of their muzzles. The odour of the killers is still a part of the morning, but the deer know that danger has gone. So they drink, and as the soft noise of their sucking whispers above the sounds of the wilderness, a silver-grey raccoon trundles business-like towards the water. He pauses a moment, close to the deer, eyes them and continues, stopping but yards away. This is Konk, raised by us three years ago. He is big, and sleek, a handsome fellow who visits here regularly. This morning he drinks, tonight he will come to fish for freshwater clams, or brownish crayfish. Soon he will waddle away to spend this day curled in a tight, furred ball deep in the recess of his den.

Out in the mid-lake the still water seems to yawn. First the slight pucker of liquid mouth as the rising of a muskrat disturbs the surface; then the parting of the 'lips' as the grey-black rat thrusts his head into the air. The yawn widens, becomes a stretch; circles broaden, speed towards shore and are broken as the rat swims northwards, staying on the surface, his body cutting a wake through the leading edge of the widest ring of water.

In the sky, a raven, a harsh black bird flapping on ragged wings, eyes keenly searching for meat leavings. A dark speck in the east is his mate, seeking also. If one finds, the other will speed to it, eager for a share. The raven croaks once, flies on, the echoes of its empty belching a seeming signal for the drumming of a pileated woodpecker. Firmly planted against an ailing poplar, the big black-and-white bird smashes at the tree with his great bill. The noise is staccato and rhythmic, pleasant.

The sun is warm now, the frost has melted. By the beaver dam there is a profusion of dead ferns and some of these are yet upright, while others are down and still others are bowed. Within these brown things three ruffed grouse scratch for meat, a perfunctory instinct for there are few insects left, but it amuses the plump, grey-and-brown birds; they have fed well already, cramming their crops with the buds of poplar and sweet-sour redness of autumn cranberries. Now they scratch, half in earnest, half in play, each watching the other in case one should find some morsel worth stealing.

Watching these animal folk on such a morning, I am again struck by the grace and beauty of them, by the magnificence of them and of their surroundings and by my own abysmal ignorance of the world in which I live. During the years that I have been attempting to repair my neglect of things natural, I have wondered whether my sudden, absorbing interest in the wilderness has not turned me into an eccentric (indeed, I suspect that some of my acquaintances have so decided on my behalf). Mornings like this banish these doubts. Squatting idly by my lake, watching it and its beings, there is no room in my mind for the idle thoughts of society. If it be eccentricity to seek and find peace, then, please Lord, make me an eccentric.

Seeing animals in their natural environment, I often remark to myself on the strange understanding that exists between the hunters and the hunted. A deer will flee instantly from a hungry wolf, detecting that the creature is hungry often before it sees the hunter. The same deer, sighting the same wolf after it has sated itself on another creature, exhibits little fear of its natural enemy. At times the scent of a wolf is enough to send the deer bolting heedlessly, eyes showing white, head held back. At other times it will stand on almost the precise spot upon which a wolf has stood, will smell its enemy, and will browse or drink unconcerned.

Why is this? The full answer escapes me yet. I can guess that the stealth of a hunting wolf is a give-away to its prey, for when full of belly the wolf lopes along unconcerned for the noise it is making. At these times the creature is not careless, it is not heedless, for wolves are ever on the alert, being perhaps the most sensitive of our wild animals, but it has no need of the slow progress of the stalk, or of the fleet speed of the open chase. To man its progress would be almost inaudible, for even when noisy by wild standards the creature is quiet by ours, but its movements are quickly picked up by the ears of the deer, organs designed for that creature's preservation. These great sound scoops are forever on the move, flicking nervously this way and that, a sort of natural radar that is never switched off. The deer may be grazing, its nostrils full of the smell of fresh grass, its eyes focused on the ground below, two of its main senses otherwise occupied; but the ears remain on guard.

Thus, this 'radar' which all the hunted possess, passes the sounds it gathers to the deer's brain. There they are classified; stealthy movement indicates the need for escape; careless, or normal pacing carries reassurance. This is reasonable, but how can a hunted creature tell by scent whether or not one of the hunters is seeking food? My explanation of this is not so ready, yet I will give my own theories, which are really little more than educated guesses; still, I feel, they are valid; I believe that the predator urge produces a chemical reaction in the bodies of those that are possessed by it. Science knows that the adrenal glands of mammals (including man) react

Female deer with doe, ears on guard.

to stimulus and discharge a substance called epinephrine, which is a hormone. (And what, some may ask, is a hormone? I must answer by quoting from the British physiologist, E. H. Starling, who defined in 1905 that a hormone is: 'Any substance normally produced in the cells of some part of the body and carried by the blood stream to distant parts [of the body] which it affects for the good of the body as a whole.' In other words, the name is given to any one of many chemical products manufactured by our bodies for our physical needs.)

Tests using man-made epinephrine show that its effects upon the body are distinct and quite varied. The blood pressure rises, the heart beats faster; there is an increase in body-sugar (glucose) in the blood and a decrease of glycogene (sugar-making substance) in the liver; the blood becomes more readily clotted; the skin becomes pale because the blood arteries become narrower; the pupils of the eyes become smaller and the muscles which make our hair 'stand on end' contract also and produce goose pimples. All these effects occur naturally in the body when fear, excitement, desire—in other words, emotion—grip it. It is believed that the discharge of extra epinephrine into the blood (the hormone is released constantly in small supplies by the adrenal glands) was designed by nature to help the body co-ordinate its activities to better effect during emergencies, to help it to fight, kill or escape.

These are scientifically known reactions. Are there others we do not yet know about? Does the body, a veritable chemical factory, produce a skin discharge which a keen-scenting creature can smell? I believe it does (but don't quote me to a scientist as a scientist will want proof!). Why do I believe this? In the first place because I have spent many hours watching the hunters and the hunted and have seen reactions which can hardly be explained by anything else; I have myself experienced the epinephrine stimulus; I have myself been a predator and have known fear. But mostly I have come to accept this belief from analyzing the reactions caused by the extra discharge of epinephrine by the adrenal glands. Let us take a look at these:

First, the blood pressure rises. This is necessary when total body action is desired, for the unusual body movements use up more energy and thus more blood is needed to 'feed' the muscles. The heart beats faster; logical again, for if more blood is needed and speeded to the body by an increase in blood pressure, it follows that the heart, our pump, must work faster (and our lungs, too) to supply the extra demand. Now the pupils of the eyes become smaller; so as to concentrate vision? Taking the elementary principles of photography, we know that the larger the aperture of our camera lens, the smaller will be the area of sharpness and that the smaller the aperture, the greater the area of sharpness. So, in the eye, when the pupil becomes smaller, the sharper the vision. Now the blood. Why does it clot more easily? Simple. If the hunter is injured he will bleed, but if his blood is stimulated to faster clotting by epinephrine, he will bleed less, and, of course, this is even more important for the hunted—if he manages to get away wounded!

As to the increase of glucose, this is almost elementary. The body 'burns' sugar. The faster it moves the more it 'burns,' the more the system must manufacture. Sugar is the fuel, epinephrine is the production stimulator. And what about those 'goose pimples'? Now I take a guess…have you ever noticed how a dog's hackles rise when he's angry or afraid? He looks fierce, those risen hackles add an extra touch of ferocity to his stance. This happens to man, as well, but man has forgotten how to snarl properly, and he has rubbed off most of his body hair with clothing, so that he just gets 'goose pimples' which do not do a thing for him other than to proclaim that he is in a deep funk, or cold!

I come now to the last emotional stimulus created by epinephrine, one which I neglected to enter into my first listing. If you have ever been really excited, or scared to death, you will recall experiencing a peculiar feeling in your stomach. We know this sensation by many slang terms: colliwobbles, tummy flip, cramps, a sinking feeling. It matters not what we call it, the reason for it is simple. When faced by sudden action, the body's number one defences are its muscles: to run with, to strike with, to bite with, to look with, to jump with…they need extra blood, as I have said, and they get it. But in such moments of crises, the stomach becomes a passenger. It is normally slow-moving in its functions, it has no defensive or aggressive role to play, therefore it can do with much less nourishing blood. So epinephrine goes to work on the muscles serving the stomach, intestines and liver and exerts on them a reaction opposite to that which it has exerted on the body muscles; these it has relaxed, allowing more blood to reach them; but it tightens the muscles serving the internal organs, decreasing the flow of blood. Hence 'that sinking feeling.'

It is quite a busy, complicated hormone, this epinephrine, and one that has not yet been fully analyzed. As to its parent, one of the adrenal glands, there is much still mysterious about it. But after studying the properties and effects of just one of the many hormones discharged by these glands, I lean heavily towards the belief that they (or perhaps some other body glands?) do produce an odorous discharge, or induce a chemical change which causes such a discharge upon the skin, which is detected by the sensitive smell of hunted creatures. You've heard the old saying: 'The things you see when you haven't got a gun!' To that one would add: the things you *don't see* when you *have* got a gun!

ONE AFTERNOON in early autumn I wandered aimlessly to the lake, the ten-minute journey protracted to an hour by frequent pauses. First I stopped to watch a porcupine as it browsed on late grasses. The creature was upwind from me and my steps were muffled by the moss, soft and replete with moisture, so that my approach went unnoticed by the spiny herbivore. It lay under a downed pine, using the trunk and the dry, sharp branches for protection, for even though these animals are normally fairly safe in the wilderness, owing to their terrible barrier of barbed quills, still they are cautious.

Seen close-to, a porcupine looks docile despite its array of armament. Its rounded head and blunt nose; its seemingly-vacant, shoe-button eyes and its slow movements lend gentleness to its appearance. And gentle it is, if it is not disturbed. Molested, it will raise its bristles and, if it can, will make off at a clumsy trot, seeking safety in the nearest tree. Persistent interference will halt it, where it will remain at bay, presenting its rear to the enemy, that rear which is armed with the short, muscular tail that is plentifully studded with its most powerful quills. If a hunter circles the creature, seeking an opening, the porcupine swivels on its front legs, revolving its body so that its chief weapon is aimed constantly at the attacker, while its relatively-unprotected head is safely tucked out of harm's way between the front legs.

On this afternoon the porcupine I was watching had no need to flee or resort to defence tactics. It munched grass, for not until frost kills the ground vegetation does this eater of trees leave the ground and commence his feeding on the bark and branch tips of the pines and poplars, its main winter diet in my forest. As I watched it, I recalled some of the fables that surround this creature.

Not the least of these concerns its credited ability to throw its quills at an enemy, using them as darts to pierce unwary animal, or human, from 'yards away.' Of course this is all nonsense! The tale was born I know not when and is as accurate as the theory, advanced in Britain in 1703 by a 'Learned Person,' which accounted for the habits of bird migration with the outrageous claim that birds passed the winter on the moon, taking sixty days to cover a one-way trip! I do not know how this 'Learned Person' arrived at his theory, but I can guess how the originator of the thrown-quill story came by his fable.

Porcupines shed their quills regularly (though not all at one time) and now and then, if one or two loose quills are about ready to fall out when the creature jerks his tail, these may be launched with enough force to carry them up to six feet away. It is possible that some early trapper got too close to a porcupine one day and one of these loose quills hit him point first. But if this did happen, all he got was a minor pinprick and a fright which he passed on to his contemporaries and which has lasted until the present day.

Another fable surrounding the porcupine concerns its breeding habit. This has given rise to a joke which, whilst intended as satire, is closer to the truth than its originators ever intended. It is contained in this riddle: How do porcupines breed? The answer is: carefully. Which is quite true, for the creatures must exercise care while mating. Much speculation has surrounded this necessary and natural function of the porcupine, and I have listened to old trappers debate this issue back and forth, some claiming that the breeding function presents no problems, others adhering stoutly to the belief that the male must become impaled upon the female's quills. In fact, both cases occur, but the porcupine (to banish forever at least one false impression) mates as other mammals do.

As usual, Creation's ways of solving problems are at once complex and simple in this case: complex, because of the muscle mechanism furnished the porcupine which allows full control over the quills; simple, because the female folds back her quills tightly, sheathing them in her fur so smoothly that they present little danger to the questing male. Occasionally, though, a male is wounded during the breeding act, but I have never heard of severe injury.

Then there is the other 'riddle'; are baby porcupines born head first so that the backwards sloping bristles do not injure mother during birth? The answer: it does not matter which way the babies emerge into the world. They are born 'in a cowl,' that is, fully enclosed in the birth sack. The mother eats away this membraneous bag and frees her infant, which is about eleven inches long, weighs about eight ounces and is already dressed for battle. Its quills are barbless, as far as the naked eye or the human fingers can detect. I have never examined them under a microscope, so I do not know if the barbs, hard to feel even in the quills of an adult, are already formed or not. At any rate, these quills are tough and very sharp as soon as they are dry, which takes, I believe, about an hour.

The creature I watched on that afternoon was a male. He must have been quite hungry, for when I continued on my walk, passing some ten feet from him, he paused only long enough to make sure that I was not approaching him, then he returned to his munching. A week earlier Joan and I had seen him (or one of his

cousins?) perched in a poplar beside the beaver canal that leads
into the lake, a black ball of fur enjoying the evening sun on his
perch twenty feet up.

My next stop during that walk to the lake was only some fifty
yards farther on, beside a greyish-brown mushroom some four
inches in diameter which was being devoured by a large slug. The
mushroom, a broad-gilled *collybia*, is a delicacy of insects and mol-
luscs and this one was firm and fleshy, evidently delicious to the
palate of the slimy, two-horned creature that had already taken several chunks out of it. I photographed them both and moved on,
now following a game trail through lowland that was dressed
mostly with young red pines and ageing poplars. At one of these I
stopped again. It was a tree of ample girth with a forked crown,
which had been holed by age and time and insects and wet and
birds, and now, I suspected, served as sanctuary to a raccoon.
I decided that one day soon I would climb the tree to see if this
was, indeed, a raccoon den.

The plaintive call of a catbird next attracted me. I searched for
it in a tangle of willows and hazels, hearing its voice and its movement, but at first unable to catch a glimpse of it. Then the outline
of its brown body emerged for a moment, hesitated, and disappeared again. The call continued, and its amazing similarity to the
distress call of a lost kitten reminded me of the first time I had
heard it, when I spent fifteen minutes searching for the puss only
to find the dark-capped relative of the mocking-bird. The one I was
now watching played hide and seek with me for a few minutes,
then became tired of the game and flew off.

I moved on, entering now the environments of the lake, near the
canal, built by beavers to allow safe swimming to their food trees:
here was marshy land overgrown with willow, intermixed with the
ubiquitous poplar, and salted here and there with shrubby white
pines. Now I paused to look at a peanut shell, wondering…what had
brought it here? It came from one of our feeders by the cabin, or
was given by Joan or me to one of our squirrels. It had been carried
over a quarter of a mile away from the site of the gift. Inspection of

the empty shell showed me that a red squirrel had eaten this one. How did I know? Because of the way it was neatly holed at each end, where the sharp cutting teeth of the squirrel had removed a cap from each point. A jay, perennial robbers of the squirrel's hoard, would have smashed the shell with its hard black beak; a raccoon would not have bothered to carry it away from the cabin, but would have crushed it clumsily and extracted the bits of smashed nut; a chipmunk would have taken it to its underground storehouse. Why did I think a red squirrel had brought it here to eat? Why not one of its black cousins? Again, the manner of its opening. The black squirrels are less patient, less neat than their smaller relatives. If a black had eaten this nut, the shell would have been stripped off piecemeal, leaving at most only one half whole.

The peanut shell now trailed behind me as I stopped to look at a recent beaver cut. An ailing poplar had been felled, its head landing in the beaver canal, its trunk suspended a few feet by some fibre threads that still joined it to the stump. The teeth marks were clean, and had I the patience, I believe I could have counted every-one of them. The inside of the trunk, at its lower end, had been hollowed by carpenter ants and already a woodpecker had been at work, drilling for the creatures that provide most of its food. I walked out on the tree trunk and squatted on it, over the water, while I photographed the debris-laden canal. Then back to shore, detouring around a wet spot and following a trail to my fording place, where two old trees spanned the canal and allowed me to cross to the rocky height that surrounds the lake proper.

On the rocks on this, the northwest side, there are few tall trees. Willows grow, and stunted poplars, and sumac, and grasses and, of course, mosses of many kinds. Here is the nesting plateau of the night hawks, those misnamed insect eaters who swoop so gracefully in the evening sky, the males, in spring, diving and popping their miniature sound barrier as they descend steeply, brake quickly with their wings and come out of their dive, the boom of their feat sounding rather like the noise made when two thick rubber bands are plucked suddenly.

At last I reached the lake. At first its surface seemed empty of life. The lilies still showed, filling the water with yellow and with white and with the shiny, deep green of their wide leaves. Threading through the veritable underwater forest of stems were the beaver runs, the areas that had been chewed free of the rope-like stems by the beaver, both as food and as a means of easier navigation under and above water. I paused by the rocky 'beach,' the drinking place of so many creatures, and there I found the remains of a muskrat. What had killed it? Fox, wolf, bobcat, mink? The wilderness kept this secret as the kill was about three days old and the granite left no traces of the killer. A tail wrenched from the carcass was bleached into greying rot where the scaly skin and sparse hair of the rat had been ripped away. The skull grinned small from the severed neck, picked clean by the scavengers; the ribs littered the ground, some whole and whitish, fleshed of their last bits of matter, others broken where strong teeth had crunched them. A few bits of skin and grey fur, a sprinkling of loose hair and fur sticking to the rock, that was all. And even these all, these poor morsels would be gone before two more sunsets graced the area.

Out on the water, movement. A duck, head down, pointed bottom aiming at the sky. A wood duck, a female. She raised, clacked gently with her beak at something she had retrieved from the murky water and paddled on through the lily leaves. She was beautiful to watch, graceful, easy of motion. Another pause, down went the neck and head to disappear under water, but the body remained horizontal this time. A moment, two, and the head came up into the air once more, water dripping from the working beak. Now a drake of the same species emerged from the reeds, and if the duck be termed beautiful, what adjective can one use to describe the pre-moult radiance of the wood duck drake?

Did the Creator, concerned with the fleeting life of the rainbow, decide to preserve its colours more tangibly by giving them to one of his creatures? If he did, the wood duck was his choice. Pure, dazzling, magnificent beauty irridesces in the plumage of the wood duck male. But having said this, how more can I describe the undescribable? Let me try, though language must fail to capture the fullness of this water bird whose Latin-Greek name, *Aix sponsa*, signifies: 'a waterfowl in wedding raiment.' His beak is the hue of translucent ruby centre-etched in white, edged in orange; his eyes twin, glowing gems of garnet shade, around both of which are patches of fluorescent green that travel upwards to the head, and white ribbons of feathers that dip backwards to form a trailing tuft. A white finger on each side of the face points upwards, separating the green from similar purple patches that also blend upwards into the 'hairline' and are rounded at their lower bases. The white fingers dip down into the white chin, lean backwards and become a half-collar of white that partly-bands the neck, close to the join of the head. Now the neck and breast and shoulders burst into mauve-copper radiance polka-dotted with white; this fades slowly as it travels along the duck's keel-line and stomach, both a white-grey salted by copper. On each shoulder, a slash of white followed by a similar shading of blue-black. The wings, folded, are a panoply: mauve, bronze, lavender, red, fawn, purple, white. Two fawn drumstick patches are trimmed with white that gives way to the yellow of legs that shines in many hues. But these are only words, they cannot do justice to the stupendous array of blended rainbow that is the wood duck male in spring and early summer—and sometimes even into the early autumn.

By contrast, the female of the species is a plain Jane, yet she is still a beauty in her own right, dressed in her garments of light greens and whites and greys and coppers, her eyes encased in white sachets and her chin greying to white. She has the white, on her bluish beak, of her spouse, but this is smaller, and while the base of his beak is trimmed in orange-yellow, hers is edged in glowing white. They are a pair worth beholding—these wood ducks. Is it any wonder that I spent so long on that afternoon watching their carefree feeding on the surface of my small lake?

As their unscientific name implies, these water birds nest in the woodlands, expropriating the nest of a pileated woodpecker, or a squirrel, or enlarging a hollow in a diseased tree. There, up to fifty feet from the ground, the female lays between ten and fifteen white eggs. She sits on them, leaving her partner to his own devices. When the hatchlings are already downy and their wing feathers beginning to show, they climb up the inside of the nest, aided by extremely sharp claws, and hesitate there while the mother calls to them from the ground. Then, by ones and twos, they launch themselves towards her, fluttering wildly in a flight that hardly merits that title; it is more like a controlled drop. The baby ducks will not again take to the air until their wing feathers are full grown. The duck then leads them to the water and there they remain until the southward migration flight in the autumn.

Of course, any creature that is so beautiful as the wood duck is marked for early death. The bird, just too lovely for its own good, was almost exterminated from the wilds of this continent. The drake is, naturally, easy to see during the height of his colour phase and, because the birds habituate the forest, they are slower marks for the hunter's gun. Then, too, they seem to have more confidence than good sense and even a clumsy hunter can bag a sitting duck. So these beauties of our wilds, while now evidently safe from extinction, are still uncommon and they are no more seen in the great numbers that once flew over this land. I shudder as I write this for it is now autumn and men with guns will soon be out again, seeking to mangle these marvellous birds.

Resting upon a piece of granite watching the ducks and feeling the warmth of sun upon my shoulders, I became a part of the wilderness. I like practising this art. The body is there, often-as-not plainly in the open, but the mind escapes, becomes a roving thing. The body remains unmoving, as dead, while the mind romps. The discomforts of immobility mean nothing at these times of complete freedom; the limbs stiffen as the flowing blood becomes sluggish, the feet (if the body be erect) become wooden, the buttocks (if the body be sitting) are flattened, brittle muscles. In this repose, the only mobile parts of the body are the eyes; these and the ears and the sense of smell continue working, feeding the mind. At such times wonders appear to the man who gives himself fully to the forest.

The wilderness becomes truly alive. Man is no longer a clumsy intruder, but a part of the world of primitive things, of a primeval system working as it must have done before the mind of humanity developed the power to dominate all other creatures. At times, the forest is a place of silence so intense that the sudden snapping of a small, dry twig echoes like a pistol shot. At other times it rages, whipped into howling fury by the winds, drubbed into audible protests by the pelting gouts of rain; on other occasions it achieves an in-between mood: the scurrying of squirrels, the buzzing of insects, the distant noise of a larger creature walking fearlessly along a game trail. And yet these are only three broad moods of the wilderness, that place of a thousand faces and a thousand, thousand emotions.

THREE

ONE AFTERNOON IN OCTOBER I turned off the lake path to walk through an area of tall poplars and slender red maples. It was a blustery day given to sudden rain squalls and the sky was in a fractious mood, now smiling and blue, as quickly sullen and dark. The cloisters of tall trees with their leaves of many colours captured my imagination. Standing amongst them I felt I was in the presence of pure creative art. Fingers of sunshine slanted downwards, passing through the tousled heads of poplar and maple, giving full tone to the leaves that still fluttered on them. Framed against the blue and white and grey of the sky, this canopy of leaf and branch was akin to the wonders of sun bursting through the stained-glass windows of some great cathedral. On the forest floor a different scene, yet one as marvellous. Fallen leaves of yellow and scarlet, brown ferns, nearly-black loam; mosses, spongy now, and vivid green; the narrow brook that carries the lake's overflow to the river reflecting the full panoply of colour as it inched musically on its way. And the shadows, tall and thick, slender and stunted; grey shadows, and black shadows, and shadows that were little more than etchings. And then the shrews…

Twin squeals of pure rage directed me to the tiny participants in one of the strangest and deadliest duels I have ever witnessed in the wilds, though it took me a moment or two to locate the furious combatants among dead leaves in the lea of a rock, some ten paces from where I was standing. There are several varieties of shrews in Canada; these belonged to the fiercest of the tribe, the poisonous short-tailed shrew. Little blue-grey creatures of scant four inches long, including their stumpy tails, with typical shrew features, pointy of nose, short of limb with ridiculously small feet and soft, silken fur, they were little waspish fellows, almost earless, with poor sight, sharp teeth and a temper so reckless and short that, by comparison, the ferocious wolverine is a mild sluggard.

I had been still long enough to assure them that it was safe to leave their dens and continue with the non-stop business of hunting, and fate brought the two face to face beside the mossy clump of granite. When I spotted them they were already hard at it, moving with such speed that at first I could not distinguish more than a blur of greyness. Then, they broke body contact for an instant and eyed each other wickedly, only to launch themselves simultaneously into a new attack. Their squeals were shrill incantations of hatred, reedy and thin, perhaps, but yet almost fearful in timbre. And they filled the air continuously, causing me to marvel that such tiny creatures could expend so such savage energy in a no-quarter fight and yet find breath enough to articulate their primordial battle cry.

The fight progressed over an area that was no greater than the space occupied by the spread of two human hands. Within this miniature amphitheatre the shrews feinted, darted in to slash, or locked in ferocious embrace only to break away and renew their rapier-thrusts with incredible, eye-baffling speed. Three minutes the combat lasted, when one shrew slumped on the leaves, mortally struck. In a trice, his opponent was on top of him and droplets of blood dribbled out of the prostrate shape to deepen the stain of autumn leaves. The winner ate his victim, right down to the tail tip, and the meal was consumed in perhaps five minutes (I was too fascinated to check my watch). Then the killer took time out to enjoy a leisurely toilet, scrubbing at his fur, licking at one or two small wounds, and actually combing himself with his sharp claws. This done, he ambled away, leaving in his wake some blood and a few shreds of flesh and sinew and some tiny clumps of bluish fur.

Three hundred years or so ago, man knew that the saliva in the mouth of a shrew was poisonous, but this was knowledge by observation during a time when the painstaking collection of scientific fact was not even a yearling art. Slowly man emancipated and science began to catalogue known, proven, indisputable evidence. Nobody, it seems, paid much heed to the stories of shrew

poison and these early reports were relegated to the category of folklore. 'Old wives tales,' said the men of learning, and thus the matter rested until recent times. Then, perhaps because a biologist became bitten by a shrew and felt the sharp burn of the little creature's spittle, tests were made and it was 'discovered' that the old fable was, indeed, a fact.

The effect of this poison is much like that of snake venom, particularly that of the hooded cobra, though not as potent and in lesser quantity. Yet it can induce stupor in small creatures by entering the bloodstream and slowing the heart action and the breathing of animals infected by it. Death does not normally accompany this stupor, but it is inevitable, nevertheless, for the tiny killer has an insatiable appetite. Just as soon as its victim is nicely 'knocked out,' it tears it apart and devours it. Most effective poison-spit is that of the short-tailed shrew, but the saliva of the long-tailed variety is yet powerful enough to partially cripple the shrew's victims.

Tests with this poison proved that a minute portion of substance extracted from ground salivary glands of the short-tailed shrew could kill mice weighing an ounce. Further tests revealed that there is enough poison in these glands to kill more than two hundred mice. In laboratory tests, of course, relatively larger and purer doses of the poison were used on experimental mice, which reacted more quickly and with more severe symptoms than the natural victims of the small killers.

Weight-for-weight and ferocity-for-ferocity, the little shrew, a creature that hardly weighs one ounce, is proportionately more aggressive, more savage, and has a greater need for food than the wolverine, a creature well-known for its fighting abilities and enormous appetite. Indeed, it is fortunate that the shrew is so small, for it will pursue, attack and kill anything below the scale of a weasel, hesitating not to fling itself at creatures twice its weight and size. Nature made it so; it was imbued with bounding, swift energy, a nervous temperament and a capacity for controlling pest species. It is one of man's best allies in the fight against mice and harmful insects. But, in following its natural functions, the shrew burns up great amounts of energy and any creature as small, with such a tiny capacity for storing energy, must, of necessity, replenish its lost strength at frequent intervals; hence the shrew's fierceness and its seemingly-insatiable appetite. Yet, such are the ways of Creation, the very capacities of the shrew work against it! It can (and does) eat its own weight in victims every three hours of the day and night—if it can find enough victims. And the very energy that drives it to this blood-thirsty massacre is responsible for curtailing the shrew's life. At one year, the shrew is getting old; at eighteen months (if it survives that long, for it has many enemies) it is likely to die of senility, an old, old animal.

As to its eating habits, the little shrew will try anything! Vegetable or animal, name it and the shrew eats it. Naturally, as is so with all of us, it has its favourite foods, and carrion is one of them. The more rotten, the better the shrew likes this form of meat, and maggots are extra titbits to tickle its palate. Thus, it helps clean up the wilderness and, in-between this form of diet, it devours moths, earthworms, beetles, grasshoppers, the larvae of flies, centipedes, slugs, snails and even lizards. Mice are another delicacy, though adults of this species are often too alert for the shrew.

Often I watch these small warriors as they ceaselessly scurry in search of food and once I found a nest with young. It had been built inside a dead tree, and the mother had gathered together a ball of dried leaves twined with grasses. The whole structure was about seven inches around with the nest chamber some two inches across. Inside there were eight infinitesimal, pink beings, each no larger than a human thumbnail, their weight so impossibly little that I know not if it has ever been recorded. As an estimate, I would say that all of those tiny beings placed simultaneously upon a scale would not have weighed more than one half of an ounce. But shrews grow as they live, fast.

One week after birth the babies start acquiring their furry coats; in two weeks they are respectably clothed; in three weeks their eyes open and the mother evidently considers them old enough to start foraging for themselves. She weans them, taking perhaps one more week for this procedure, then out they go to hunt for their dinners, while she gets ready to begin a new family, for shrews have from two to four litters in one year.

Now the youngsters are exposed to their natural enemies: the hawks and owls, the weasels and skunks and foxes and bobcats, and even wolves, at times. Twin musk glands, as stinky as those of the weasel, if much smaller, make these little beings unpalatable to some predators, yet, when food is scarce in the wilderness even a stinky meal of shrew is better than a shrunken, aching belly.

Much of what I have recounted of the short-tailed shrew applies to his relatives, though these are not as poisonous. But one of his cousins, the water shrew, which abounds around my lake, needs a little space of his own in this narrative. Often, during our early acquaintance with our lake, Joan and I would be startled and puzzled by hearing a quick squeak followed by a plop as some small creature dived into the water at our coming. Then, one day, I had the patience to wait, unmoving, beside the lake bank at the spot where the plop had taken place. For almost ten minutes I remained still, watching as the disturbed water slowly settled, then up came a pointy nose and the shoulders of a water shrew. In a moment it was busy amongst the lily pads, feeding on insects. I moved and the squeak was uttered and down popped the little shrew, almost faster than my eyes could follow its actions.

In clear water a diving shrew can be easily seen, for its fur traps numerous air bubbles that give it buoyancy and help it to swim underwater or crawl along the bottom looking for insect larva or fish eggs. At times, the creature appears cloaked in a gown of pure pearls as it swims along, at other times it seems dressed in silver. Surfacing, the air bubbles disappear, and though the outer fur (the guard hairs) be wet, the shrew's 'woollen underwear' is bone dry, since the air bubbles also serve to make the creature waterproof. It is fascinating to watch one of these little chaps underwater, but it is even more intriguing to see one scurry across

the surface of a quiet lake. Incredible as it at first seems, the little animal actually is able to walk on water, using air bubbles trapped under its feet rather like aquatic roller skates!

The shrew is probably closer to the original ancestor of all mammals (including man) than any other species of creature living on earth in this century. If evidence of evolution can be accepted, then the shrew, or a creature much like it that lived in the treetops of prehistory, sired the mammals that today live on earth. Be this as it may, the shrew is one of man's greatest natural allies, and although it does at time consume some birds and their eggs and kill a portion of animals and birds useful to man, creatures of the family *Soricidae*, which comprises five separate groups, do more good than they do harm, albeit they are blood-thirsty little fellows with few characteristics calculated to endear them to the average human. On the whole, we tend to love only those animals that are 'soft and cuddly' and have 'nice habits'; though I have not yet been quite able to define just what is meant by that last!

A WALK BY THE LAKE in autumn. A quiet walk, leisurely strides punctuated by frequent stops to look and listen and smell, while the creatures of the wilderness live their lives undisturbed by a roaring age of space travel. These walks teach me a great deal of the wilderness and its people, but not nearly enough!

A NIGHT OF AUTUMN. Frost glistens in the moonlight; fine, shimmering dust particles of ice extracted from the air by the cold. Overhead the stars, a veritable explosion of blue-green dots winking erratically against the dark blueness of space. Adding to the light of a half moon, the glow of the Aurora Borealis burns a mystic roadway across the heavens. The lake is a place of intense shadows and gleaming reflections, dancing, multi-coloured beams of light that convert the dull little spot into an enchanted lagoon.

The bullfrogs are silent. The tree frogs and the leopard frogs and their relations are now cold, still shapes pressed into leaf mould or freezing mud, asleep for another season, their departure from this place noticeable because of its silence. In a big white pine at the south-east corner of the lake, an owl hoots. It is a great horned owl, the tiger of the night skies, whoo-hooing to himself in bass voice as he perches expectant upon a thick, dead limb.

Gentle ripples glide over the surface of the lake as the passage of an unseen beaver furrows the smoothness of quiet water. Now a splash draws attention to itself, a quiet sound, midway up lake, made by a muskrat as it dives, fearful of the deep resonance of the big owl. A loping hare, its coat just acquiring the white of winter dress appears silhouetted atop of a rock near the owl's pine. Why does the foolish creature stand thus? Did it not hear the voice of its killer? There it is, a long-eared, nervous being of this forest, half-sitting, half-crouched, gripped by the indecision of its own doom.

A swift shadow floats briefly over the land. The owl is sailing in, talons already spread, legs stretched, reaching for the warm softness of the snowshoe hare. The foolish one reacts too late, leaps twisting in a frenzy of fear, is impaled upon the gripping talons of the owl. A thin scream of pain and terror escapes the hare; the great shadowy shape of the hunting owl is stilled over the corpse. The hunter's round head, its 'ears' showing like miniature devil's horns, twists slowly in seeming fully circle as the bird, its keen vision handicapped by eyes that are fixed in their sockets, searches the night for...what? For danger? For more prey? Perhaps it is still listening to the cry of death of its victim, a sound gone now, disappeared into the labyrinths of space, yet still felt here because of the intense silence it has created. The owl snaps its rapacious beak; the sound is like the clapping of human hands. The bird eats, pulling, tearing, cracking the skull; trepanning the bone with its powerful jaw-vice, exposing the warm, grey brains. The owl eats the brains, pauses an instant as though tempted to eat more of its kill, then rises ponderously from the rock, winging silently into the night, leaving the carcass of the hare for others to finish. Hunting is good tonight, the big bird does not now eat for hunger's sake, but through habit, and a special fondness for new-killed brains.

Over the lake silence, and darkness, and moonlight, and great grotesque shadows that move. One minute, two minutes thus, then a new noise; a small chirping sound issuing from the arms of a dead poplar that still stands by the water's edge. Three tiny calls, melodious, bird-like; and the fluffy fawn shape of *Glaucomis volans* emerges from a hole in the tree trunk. The flying squirrel is made of fluid motion. Out into the night it glides, slides swiftly upwards, to the topmost branch and launches its small body through space, four legs spread wide, the skin flap of its sail taut and wind-filled as it floats into the arms of a pine. Again silence.

Stealthy pads move along the lip of the beaver dam as the red fox is drawn to the carcass of the hare. The scent of warm blood fills the creature's nostrils, carrying the message of death. But caution is needed, for perhaps a more powerful killer is even now feeding from the hare's body. So the fox steals silently over the mud and sticks of the dam, easing his supple body in and out of the willows and young birches that jostle each other on the south side of the lip. The dam curves, a sturdy bridge in crescent shape, a hundred yards long, anchored at its eastern end against the roughness of blue granite. Upon this rock the fox stops, mouth

A red fox at The Place, eating food put out daily.

slightly agape, revealing a glimpse of pink tongue and the eager drool that is dripping from the black lips. The pointed ears are strained forward, the black, shiny nostrils quiver with eagerness as the aroma of blood is inhaled deeply into the lungs; but the red body is kept in check while the keen brain translates the messages delivered to it by the senses. Then at last the fox is allowed freedom, for only the scent of death lies ahead. The fox eats.

Half-a-mile away timber wolves are moving. Three grizzled beasts, tall, rawboned, swift and powerful are tracking a white-tail buck with relentless patience and endurance of their kind; unhurried, silent. The deer breaks cover near the feeding fox and the red creature streaks for the shelter of dense underbrush, abandoning the half-eaten hare. The fox's movement startles the deer, makes it change course, so that now it turns away from the south and plunges into the dark lake waters, its dive a loud signal to the keen ears of its hunters, its progress noisy and splash-laden. There is great fear in the big, soft eyes; they show white, they roll upwards, as though trying to hide themselves in the head, which is arched backwards so that the regal beauty of antlers not yet shed becomes lost in the distorted blur of water and movement.

Here the lake is narrow and the deer soon gains the west shore. Out of the water it scrambles, revealing by its hasty, noisy progress that it is in the grip of blind panic. The water cascades from the red-fawn hair as the buck lunges upwards, gains more solid ground and crashes into the wall of forest. Behind it the wolves pause by the lakeshore, their noses down to the scent. Will the deer escape? The thought is framed in my mind and human emotion destroys my resolve; I was not going to interfere, yet I cannot resist. I step away from the gnarled balsam that has given me concealment and I call out to the wolves. Three broad heads lift; six brown-flecked eyes stare. I walk towards the shoreline. The wolves, turn, tarry a moment, looking at man over their shoulders, then race away, retracing their steps; perhaps intent on circling and again resuming the chase, more likely philosophically abandoning this kill and already intent on finding another.

The sentiment of man! Why did I do this thing this night? Why did I not maintain my resolve and allow the hunters a chance to eat? The law here is clear. There are those who kill and those who are killed; it is the code of the wilds, upset this night by the meddling of a human. And the spell is broken. I turn to go, for now the wilderness knows that an intruder is here and it hugs its secrets more closely to itself. Still there is pleasure left for me as I stroll along the wide pathway that leads to the highway that will take me back to my woods cabin. I do not carry a light this evening, but my feet know this path and are in no need of eyes to guide them. My eyes rest, and my nostrils work harder as they smell the night, and my ears scoop more sounds out of the air. The aroma of pine gum, the fragrance of balsam pitch, the yeasty smell of decaying leaves; now the thick odour of raccoon, the fetor, faint, of a skunk's rank scent. The whisper of pine needles, the gentle swaying of naked poplars and birches, the scurry steps of a mouse...the sounds and smells of a bush night, every one a familiar thing, a friend, yet each of them as new tonight as they were when I first discovered them.

Fourteen years have passed since that time, when I was a newcomer to this vastness of earth and rocks and lakes that is Canada. The wilderness around me was enormous, frightening; a savage, frozen place that January when I met it full-face. It stretched around me for mile after mile of forested, snow-laden earth, peopled by creatures unknown to me. And almost at once it taught me a lesson.

I was returning at dusk from a hunting trip (shooting hares for the pot) when I fancied that stealthy movement was keeping pace with my blundering progress through snow that was three feet deep in places. At first I tried to ignore it, convincing myself that my imagination was playing tricks with me; but the feeling persisted. I stopped, and the sound, if it could be called such, ceased. I moved and the feeling that I was being followed again exerted itself and I paused again, quickly. Now I knew that some creature was behind me, treading carefully, but staying on my trail.

My rifle was a .22 calibre, a useless thing, I felt, for whatever was behind me. I knew fear and tried to spit out the taste of it. I moved as quickly as I could. Still the tracker persisted. I stopped again and looked backwards and I saw the fleeting greyness of a timber wolf seeking cover behind a balsam. My adrenals pumped epinephrine into my blood and the hair on the back of my neck arose in pathetic mimicry of a killer's mane. But I was no killer then, just a human novice in a wild land with a wolf at his back, four miles of forest ahead of him and sudden fear within his bowels. I shouted, more in encouragement to myself than in hopes of scaring the wolf, and I threw myself fully at the impeding snow, my body bathed in sweat, my breath a series of noisy gasps. Rapidly I was losing control. From somewhere, perhaps the reflexes of war training, I summoned sternness and schooled myself to calm, telling myself all the while that man's greatest weapon is his brain. That's a good thought, when it is born in the safety and warmth of an armchair by the fireside; have you ever tried to believe in it when you thought real danger threatened? It is hard to do. Yet I steadied, forcing myself to return to an easy pace while the creature behind me adjusted its own progress. And then I realized that the wolf, while following me, was not gaining.

Little as I knew then of this great animal of ours, I was still sufficiently aware to realize that the wolf could have closed the distance between us in half-a-dozen bounds. The animal, then, was either afraid to attack, or was merely curious. I felt better and ashamed of my fear, and I stopped and turned and sought the grey shape. For perhaps two minutes I searched and failed to find, then the wolf, obeying some unknown whim, broke cover, stood broadside-on to me for a moment, looking me directly in the eyes, then bounded away through the snow to become swallowed by the forest. I laughed my relief and amusement. The creature had evidently been curious of the man-thing that tramped so clumsily through its country; it had followed, no doubt sucking into its nostrils the strange odour of man, its great curiosity glueing him to my heels.

Since that time I have observed many timber wolves and handled not a few. I have been followed a number of times and I have learned that man is safe from these hunters. It may be that, on occasion, driven by desperation, a wolf has attacked a man, but these instances are few and often unrecorded. Since that cold January those many years ago, I have made friends with the timber wolf and have learned to respect it and have been fascinated by its fine intelligence, its courage, its strength, its endurance. This is not a villain, but a victim, a victim of man and his fears. Such fears have shrouded the wolf in mythological evil that has condemned the poor creature to the everlasting hatred of humanity, for no other reason than that it is doing what Creation ordained it should do. It kills; it must kill. It does it well and fulfills its role in the wilderness pattern. Withal it is a noble beast with a great capacity for love; it is faithful to its kind; it is a receptacle of emotions that, guileless, are readily reflected in its eyes, in its ears and in its mouth that can smile with a charm surpassing the most winsome of human grins.

Of course the wolf is savage! It must be so, or perish. But compare this creature with man...is man not the most savage, cruel creature upon this planet? Man kills to eat also, but he has been able to secure to this cold-blooded, professional slaughter the label of 'necessity.' He says he kills cleanly and quickly and that his victims do not suffer. Then, during the most beautiful time of the year on this planet, the autumn, he sets forth with his guns to slay all. Many creatures of the wilderness are wounded and left to die a death that is lingering. Many creatures lie torn and fearful while man, lust alive in his gaze, strolls casually up to them and smiles a proud smile, then calmly lowers his gun-muzzle and shatters one more graceful life. Is this thing then, less savage, less cruel, less lustful than the natural killing of the timber wolf?

It is strange that when man kills he readily finds an excuse for his actions. When I hunted I saw nothing wrong with what I was doing and I derived great pleasure from my 'prowess.' And before that time, when my own kind were the targets of my weapon, there were few qualms of conscience for the dead of the enemy; yet, paradoxically, there was deep emotion for the friends who died a like death. This was insanity and I am aware now of the degree of this madness; but I am more deeply aware of another thing: life. I think often of the ease with which man can create death, and I compare this with the infinite, intricate process that evolves in life, that tenuous, fragile *something* that we cannot ourselves create, yet of which we are so frightfully careless. Ironically, the wilderness has taught me this, not the schooling that was imparted to me by my own kind; not the doctrines of Christianity so lavishly expended upon my small person when I was a child.

Beside my lake I see life in forms so many and different that it defies classification. Yet I try, as I did on the day when I stopped to look at a mushroom. Naturally, I had seen vast numbers of these fungi in the past; I had even learned something of them in botany classes, but until that September morning I had not truly examined a mushroom, nor thought about it in any great detail. Until then I classed this life form into two broad groups: those which were edible, and those which were poisonous. But, standing over the perfect circle of orange spotted with cream, with its smoothness and its roughness and with its bulbous stem and its creamy, velvety shirt, I saw a mushroom clearly for the first time.

It was an *Amanita muscaria* (or fly agaric), one of the most beautiful and most deadly (to man, anyway) of our wild gilled mushrooms, plants all, yet vastly different in their habits, structure and growth to the well-known green things that are all around us.

Botanically, fungi are classed as a lower order of vegetation. They belong to a large family, for some 70,000 different species of them have been classified, amongst which the best known are those we call mushrooms, which include the puffballs; club fungi; coral fungi; stinkhorns; morels; tube fungi and the agarics, or gilled mushrooms, to which the *Amanita* belongs. As is the case with all their many relatives, mushrooms lack chlorophyll, the substance that turns green and allows the higher plants to make use for their nourishment of the simple elements in air, water and earth. Because mushrooms lack this magic material they behave, in a sense, like animals, depending for their food on other living things or upon their dead bodies. So, in a sense, mushrooms are predators; they are also scavengers, helping to clean up the wilderness. Rotting wood, fallen leaves and mulch are some of the foodstuffs of the mushroom; other nourishment is secured when mushrooms become parasites, living off a live host: a tree, a plant.

When I was a boy, I used to think that mushrooms were 'born' out of cow manure that abounded in the open fields of England, an old fable still shared by some adults in this age, and, of course, quite wrong. How, then, do mushrooms reproduce themselves? They are unlike the green plants, which propagate themselves through seeds pollen-fertilized by sexual contact between the male and female parents of the species (some of which are bisexual— that is, one individual has both male and female reproductive organs). Mushrooms, however, are thought to lack the sexual elements that exist in green plants and instead of the sex-pollen-seed cycle, they manufacture minute bits of life called spores which are released when the mushroom reaches maturity. These spores, too small to be seen alone with the naked eye, are readily seen in a mass, sometimes creamy-white, at other times in any one of several colours. These tiny spores are, in a sense, eggs, in that they consist of protoplasm (living matter) encased inside a membrane.

Spores, seen in a mass, look like dust and one mushroom can produce literally billions of these infinitesimal 'eggs,' no doubt because only a very few of the spores ever find a spot suitable for 'hatching' and growing up, for Creation, while always careful with the species, is rather wasteful of the individuals. However, for those few fallen spores lucky enough to land on a good growing spot, life is a relatively simple process (if something does not kill them before they have a chance to mature). The lucky spores begin to germinate, first shooting out a minute white thread that wriggles its way into the rotten (or live) wood or into the loam of its birthplace. Now this little thread of life begins to eat. It does not chew or drink, but it absorbs nourishment from its host and begins to multiply itself, growing longer, sending out branches until it has built for itself a network of threads which now can be seen easily. This is the body of the plant, the mycelium, as the scientists call it, or spawn, as others refer to it.

Now the network must wait. Perhaps only a few weeks, perhaps months, even years. Then it is old enough and strong enough to begin to grow fruit, which at first are hardly more than little bumps in various places along the network of threads. These little knobs, getting bigger, and bigger, until they stick out from the ground or wood, are the 'buttons' of the mushroom which continue rising and unfolding themselves until they become the perfectly formed, fleshy umbrellas we all know.

At first, when little more than a rounded cap peeps out of the ground, the mushroom embryo looks rather like a single egg, but as the growth continues, twin eggs, joined together to form a waist, appear. As growth increases, the bottom egg remains underground while the top egg pushes up, and now the young mushroom splits its coat and the stalk, short yet, is visible. Later on the stalk lengthens and the original skin, carried upwards, becomes the little shirt that surrounds the mushroom just below its gills, while the bottom egg, called the cup, remains in the ground where it is anchored by fine roots. And it is in this cup that most of the mushroom's poison is stored. Some species that are deadly poison if the cup is pulled with the mushroom, become harmless if the stalk is carefully cut above the cup, leaving the poison underground (but don't experiment, mushrooms are dangerous unless they are positively identified as harmless).

September is mushroom time in my forest. By the lake and almost everywhere in this piece of wilderness abound mushrooms of all shapes, colours and sizes: orange Amanitas; brown, wrinkled morels; beautiful, blood-red *Russulas*; little brownie clusters of elfin caps; wrinkled, upward-slanting *Cantharellus*, pale coral in shade; an endless procession of fungi in their full array of delicate colours. Now the squirrels start gathering their crop. They bite through the fleshy umbrellas and carry pieces of the mushroom into the trees,

where they set them out to dry, to be collected later and transferred to their middens, the winter's vegetable supply. Possibly the inspiration was for man to follow the squirrel's way and thus preserve mushrooms for soups and stews. And the insects and birds attack the mushrooms, leaving their beak marks, or the signs of their chewing mouths, as little pinches of flesh are taken from the umbrellas. And again I am reminded of the large slug that was so busy chewing on the *Collybia*, a mushroom which at times smells faintly of anise, and at other times reeks with the odour of rot. What a feast the slug was having! It dragged itself in leisurely manner right over the top of its vast dinner, its soft chewing mouth taking a pinch here, a nip there, the while criss-crossing the mushroom cap with a glistening trail of slime. The next morning, I found that something else had ransacked what was left of the slug's dinner, perhaps a squirrel or chipmunk, and now all that remained was a shattered fragment of the stalk and a few dried bits of the gills and cap.

FOUR

Now it is late autumn on the lake, that time between the snarl of winter and the passing of the season of colour. The frost deepens, sinking an inch into the ground, coating the lake each morning with a skin of ice that does not fully retreat before the sun. The beaver are hard at it among the poplars, beginning early in the morning, working into full sun-up, starting again before dark; gnawing and biting and peeling, standing away from toppling trees to wait until the crash, then to run fatly for the water, for the sound of the crash might bring a hunting creature upon them. And then back they come, to feast on tender bark, to cut the tree into lengths and to carry these along the trail and into the water. Then to swim away with them to the area of the lodges, there to dive carrying the stick between clenched teeth, their nostrils closed by invisible valves, their loose lips meeting in the open mouth, so that no water will force its way down the throat. On the mud bottom the beavers push and shove, wedging their winter's food into the soft ooze, anchoring it there until it is needed during the time of the big cold, when the lake will be sheathed in a heavy layer of snowy ice.

Among the brown catkins, a muskrat. Fat, old; a dark male feeding on the few remaining stalks that are still tender. While his neighbours, the careful, husbanding beavers, are working long and hard to secure winter supplies, the old rat lives in a life of ease. Eating when hungry, sleeping when tired, occasionally exploring his limited world, his only concern is the preservation of himself from the teeth of the hunters. His movements amongst bullrushes are slow, his dark coat unclear behind its shield of stems.

He rears on his hind legs and rests both front paws on one of the still-juicy stalks and, steadying himself with his oval, scaly tail, he bends his sharp face to the food and bites into it. Three bites he

The beaver dam.

makes, then the catkin, weighted by its brown busby, topples down, releasing a shower of fluffy, black-tipped seeds that float away to disperse over the water. The old rat continues work on the stem. He cuts it into four sections, each some eight or ten inches long and he makes a neat pile of these little logs. He pauses a moment, eyes the remaining head, then, seemingly satisfied, he settles down to his meal, eating one stem after the other.

Above the catkins and the rat is a rock that was already ancient when earth spawned man. It rose out of its matrix and became sheared at its northern face. Now that face is green with moss and weather has chipped it in places and grooved it. Ferns grow in the grooves, and one spindly, twisted cripple of a pine. Atop this rock grows a wide, dwarf-juniper. Crouched under the cover of the juniper a small brown-streaked killer lurks. He is intent on the muskrat, his sharp features eager with the lust of blood.

The sun has bedded for this day, the evening sky but vaguely reflects its colour and the lake and the forest are bathed in the half-light that presages the coming of dark. The weasel sheltering under the juniper is out earlier than usual tonight, for he is hungry, unsated since early yesterday. He is now pondering…can he reach the old rat? And if he does, will he be able to kill it? Muskrats are fighters and they are strong; they are not the usual prey of the weasel. But hunger is pressing and the little killer knows not the meaning of fear and once, last spring, he killed a rat and feasted royally upon its blood and its meat. He remembers that kill now and he hesitates, for he carries a scar upon his right shoulder that was made when the rat's long canines raked him before he could sever his victim's jugular vein. Still the question persists…can he reach the fat creature down there in time to secure the death grip? The beady black eyes glisten with excitement, the low-slung, supple body quivers; the long, sinuous neck moves gently, undulating, while the haunches sink a little closer to the rock. Suddenly, the muskrat takes fright. He is eating the last stem, but he drops it and rushes for the water, his seemingly-clumsy body making good speed. In a moment he is gone, under a swirl of ice-filled wet mixed with a few air bubbles showing where he has dived.

The weasel is a philosopher—he has to be—and the rat's fright and escape leave him unmoved. The urge reflected in his eyes persists and he moves slowly, walking his rolling gait, tail held out stiffly, a little brush carried parallel to the ground which occasionally sweeps the rock surface. Along the flat he travels, heading east, down a slope and into a country of sere marsh grass. Now he quickens his pace and starts to bound, neck waving, little pointed ears erect, hind quarters rounded.

He hears movement. There is a pause in the killer's run while his nostrils seek that which impinged upon his hearing. One quick sniff, two. It is a white-footed mouse that is already seeking escape and the weasel launches his suppleness in pursuit. The race is short, for something has taken hold of the mouse and made it foolish, transformed it into a shaking little brown and white bundle that now cowers beside a dead fern. Why does the little creature stay there awaiting so meekly the death that must soon come to it? It is the power of the weasel that has done this thing. A strange aura generated by the killer affects many of its victims, a hypnotic trance that, at times, saps the will from its victims, many of which, like the luckless mouse, can outrun the relatively slow weasel.

It happens in a trice. The killer, if slow when running, is all flashing speed when twisting and dodging and now, in characteristic manner, it pauses for a fraction of time, long neck waving the pointed head; then, in a trice, it launches itself at the mouse and appears to wrap itself around the fearful creature, the strong, slender forelegs gripping the white-foot's body. In a second, long sharp canines sink into the mouse's throat, unerringly centred upon the big neck vein, the jugular, where the strong blood-pulse is. And the blood flows into the killer's mouth and it drinks greedily, and the mouse died as his slayer feasts upon his blood. A moment or two and the small victim is bled almost dry. Now the weasel eats the body.

It is good to have food in the belly, when hunger is a constant companion. It is better to have the belly swollen with food, hurting from it, threatening to push fresh meat back up the throat that has swallowed it. The mouse inside the belly of the weasel becomes a thing of comfort; but more meat is demanded now that the gastric juices are again busy upon substance. The weasel licks his chops, he wets his front paws and brushes his face, he carefully licks a blood-spot from his white-flecked vest. Then he sets out on the hunt again and his sinuous lope continues for ten minutes by the time standards of man. The ears listen hard, and the nostrils syphon scents and the weak eyes do their best to help, but are content to let the other two senses perform the bulk of the work. A shrew is discovered; another brief attack, and more death, and a little more meat joins the remains of the mouse in the working belly. And again the weasel washes and sets out anew. Now the dark has come full and the horned owl hoots with its deep voice and flaps lazily with silent wings and begins to drop on the weasel.

Instinct saves the little killer. By one second it avoids death, twisting in flashing speed and darting under a fallen pine. The owl lifts and wings on, patient, unperturbed by the miss, for this is the way of the hunters and there are many victims about this night.

Soon the questing talons will find a warm body in which to fasten. The weasel, too, is unperturbed. This has happened before and there is nothing to be gained by emotion; that death has again been cheated is sufficient in itself, now life must be sought, for the belly is still in need. So the weasel seeks again, and finds. And he seeks again and finds again, and is satisfied. And he turns for home, which is a remodelled chipmunk burrow lined with the fur and feathers of the dead. It is warm there, and sleep is always good in the comfort of a full belly.

EBONY NIGHT and crisp cold. The lake is silent; the forest is a place of small, rustling sounds. Overhead heavy clouds press towards earth, dropping tendrils of moisture that freeze as they settle on trees and bushes. Approaching the lake, two hunters; wolves, big creatures with broad pads and bellies shrunken with hunger, flanks leaned, bushy tails carried curled under, so that their tips rest almost against the deep chests. They are silent as they trot, for they seek the scent of deer.

A white-tail is slowly approaching the lake; a doe, old, ailing, her vitals infested with parasites, her nose choked with the larvae of botflies, so that she cannot breathe through it and instead gasps air into her lungs through gaping mouth. The doe has seen eleven autumns. She will not see another winter, for it is her time. If luck is with her this night, the wolves will find her and make her end quick; if the hunters do not reach her, death will be slow and terrible. Now she tries to drink of the ice-filled water and has not the strength to lower her neck while standing. Painfully, she kneels and reaches for liquid and drinks a little, each swallow painful.

She hears the wolves and tries to rise, but her muscles are too worn. She remains by the lakeshore, front knees bent, hindquarters stiff, her neck turned towards the hunters who know she is there and hurry, eagerness in their gaze. For perhaps one minute the scene is unchanged, then the wolves arrive to within ten feet of the deer. They stop; they test the air and fix their eyes upon their prey while the doe struggles anew to find footing.

She is almost up now. The wolves move. They separate and attack from two flanks. One seizes a hind leg and clamps razor teeth upon the tendons. The other goes for the throat, closing his jaws upon the doe's softness. In a moment the deer is down, her throat is torn, the tendons of one leg ripped out. She is dead even as she hits the ground and her tired old blood pumps out slowly, staining red the wolf that ripped the throat vein. The hunters eat, and while they are sating themselves, the fly larvae in the deer's nostrils become agitated. They are whitish, maggoty things about half an inch long and they have already detected a drop in the temperature of their nesting chamber. They move, wriggling urgently, climbing blind one over the other. Two fall out of the right nostril and lie upon the frosted ground; they jerk their plumb bodies as the cold attacks them and they grope instinctively for new shelter; but there is none and the cold kills them. They are the first of their brood to die. Soon these remaining inside the deer's nostrils will be vanquished by the frost.

The wolves lie side by side and their muzzles are steeped in the blood of the doe, and their teeth and jaws are busy as they pull and sever and crunch and chew and swallow. Now and then one wolf attempts to eat too close to its partner and savage snarls shatter the quiet; both of the creatures bare their bloodied teeth and work the growls out of their throats. But they do not attack each other and in a moment there is quiet again as each intruder returns to his portion of the prey.

Thirty yards from the wolves and their prey, sits a red fox. He is waiting his turn, fearless of the great killers who are too busy to notice him, but he takes care to remain unmoving, his body pressed close to the shelter of a balsam fir. Squatting on his haunches, with his white chest a light blur in the dark, he is all eagerness and impatience. His little black nose moves constantly as it sucks in the mouth-watering smell of a new kill. His ears are sentinel-rigid, cupped towards the sounds of the feast, his eyes unwinkingly fixed upon the wolves and the doe. For almost twenty minutes he remains thus, then the wolves rise, gorged at last, stretch their stiff muscles and lope down to the lake's edge. Cracking ice with their muzzles they drink, stretch once more, and begin to wash the blood from their bodies; the fox almost cries in his eagerness and exasperation. But at last the wolves are done and they turn from their kill.

Now is the time for the fox. Quickly he rises and slithers to the half-eaten carcass, but he has not had time to take the first mouthful when he is disturbed. He retreats, undecided; then he growls slightly and advances on his supper, for his quick nostrils have detected the cause of his disturbance. A skunk has arrived. It, too, must have been waiting for the wolves to finish their meal and it has reached the kill almost simultaneously with the fox. The two eye each other for a moment. The fox bristly, angry, his mane up, his sharp muzzle open, showing the gleaming teeth. The skunk stands stiff-legged, ready to adopt the U-position necessary for spraying her dreadful musk. But there is meat here for them both and they soon tire of their threatening stances. The fox breaks first. Slowly he crouches beside the ripped belly of the deer and begins to feed. The skunk relaxes and waddles to the neck, daintily nipping pieces of meat from it. The two feed undisturbed.

The skunk finishes first and lopes away. In another moment, the fox is done and he, too, leaves. Now the partly-eaten carcass is alone. But not for long. Tiny shapes scurry amongst the dead grasses as they approach the kill. At the head of the old doe, a white-footed mouse begins to eat. At the belly, another; two more eat of one flank. Again silence that is broken by an occasional squeak of delight. Then the great horned owl glides over and drops on one mouse and the others flee in terror. The deer is again alone.

Now the larvae that have been eating inside the deer's nostrils, and in its sinuses, and, in fact, in any cavities they could find inside the stricken creature's head, are dying. The carcass has cooled greatly and the black-banded maggots cannot stand the drop in temperature. This repulsive brood will not survive to become adult-nose botflies next spring. But, of course, there will be others like them who will live, and the *Oestridae* family of flies will continue to thrive upon the blood of their hosts.

By next spring, these flies will again zoom through the forest at speeds of up to fifty miles an hour in pursuit of deer. They are curious creatures, these botflies, yellowish to grey in colour, about half-an-inch long and hairy. The females of the species are skilled fliers and even more skilled 'bombardiers,' being able to place their eggs in the nostrils of the deer without actually alighting on their host, laying on the wing, as it were. And this while the deer is running at speed, for they are afraid of the persistent, dangerous flies and always try to avoid them.

At first the larvae are tiny, whitish in colour, with a pair of hooks in their mouths by which they fasten themselves inside the linings of the deer's nostrils and nasal passages. Slowly they develop into fat maggots, still yellow-white but now with a dark band around their bodies. Some ten months later, between the following spring and early summer, the mature maggots leave the deer by the simply process of letting themselves fall, or allowing themselves to be sneezed out of the deer's nostrils. Now they are about one inch long, their bodies flat on the bottom. On the ground, they pupate and become flies whose main function in life is to mate and then seek a new host for the vile little eggs they carry inside of their repulsive bellies. If the deer is strong enough and if the fly only lays a few eggs upon its nostrils, the animal survives with minor discomforts. If the infestation is heavy, the deer suffers greatly and if it be an old animal, already weakened by other parasites and by age, it will be doomed by the yellow-nose fly.

This has been the fate of the old doe, released from further miseries by the mercy-slashes of the timber wolves. She has lived her life, now her death brings needed energy to other creatures who live beside my lake. At this moment the old doe's remains rest, their juices falling on to the frozen earth, melting some of it or pooling on the ice, ready to put fresh vitality into the soil on which they now rest just as soon as winter flees and the ground is again ready for nourishment.

So goes this night of death. Again quiet, dark still, cold; an interlude of forest stealth not often seen by man. And suddenly a faint,

shrill squeak. It is the last cry of a white-footed mouse, discovered and killed by the weasel, who is again hungry. The odour of death has coaxed the weasel to this place and it has stumbled upon a mouse and tarried just long enough to kill and eat, for opportunity cannot be wasted in the wilderness. Now it hurries with its bounding run, eager to sink sharp teeth into the remains of the deer.

Fifteen inches of supple weasel crouch beside the front quarters of the deer and begin the feast. The little brute is alone, a gourmet faced by a seemingly-unending banquet. This is happiness, a feast for dreaming, a meat eater's paradise; so let us leave him there for a time while we look more closely into the life of *Mustela*, said to be the most blood-thirsty of all the mammals.

Three Aprils ago, the weasel was born in a remodelled chipmunk den after his mother had eaten its builder. He was one of ten kits; a pink, toothless, wrinkled mite about two inches long that weighed perhaps one ounce and a half. He screamed powerfully just as soon as his mother's birth struggles pushed him out into the world, and he lay still, in-between outbursts, while his mother birthed her remaining babies. Then he was licked and dried, and he nuzzled into her belly and grasped one of her small dugs and suckled lustily, the first feed of his hungry life.

During the seven days the dark tips of his chocolate-brown coat began to show and his scream was more hearty. One more week and he and his brothers and sisters were able to wobble about the chamber on little legs that just would not become steady. Now they were housebroken, leaving their bedroom with their funny little stagger to go and relieve themselves a few feet away, guided by their already-alert noses and ears, for their eyes were still unseeing. At this time, some mock battles began to take place between them and the strong, lithe movements of their bodies were marvels in things so small.

Five weeks passed. Inside the chipmunk burrow, the young kits popped open their eyelids and were able to see, though only darkness met their gaze. By their movements and the fights that broke out amongst them, their mother knew this was their time.

She waited for night, then led them outside and began their training. Two hours later she led them back to their den, but now she refused their questing lips. After turning from them for some minutes she left them alone, racing out of her earthen tunnel and into the night, leaving the kits hungry and irritable, so that fighting became noisy.

Sleep came to the young weasels at last. In a chamber rank with the smell of carrion and alive with the fetor of their own musk, the kits snored, blissful little creatures whose nostrils noticed not the stench of their quarters. Why was this? Well, Creation being what she is, there is usually more than one answer to any of her puzzles. So it was with the weasels, as it is with all creatures that smell, including man. The strong odour of a weasel den is offensive to human nostrils, educated as they have become to sweeter aromas of this world, but, to a weasel, this is only natural. But there is yet a thing which helps all scenting noses to work more efficiently. Inside the nose of each of us there are some special cells. Scientists call them chemoreceptor cells, using their dry language to lightly brush over a wonderful thing. In fact, this term only implies that these cells are sensitive to certain chemical substances. Thus, we can smell all manner of things, and taste them, for similar cells live in the mouth. In the nose, these cells are hidden high up in the nasal cavity, in a place not disturbed by the incoming rush of air that we breathe. A proportion of the 'smell bits' that we suck into our nostrils enter the smell chamber and are trapped there to become dissolved in the mucus which protects the cells.

These sensitive cells have free ends which grow into the mucus layer and these ends become stimulated by the chemicals which furnish 'body' to all things, minute portions of which are constantly lost into the air and form the basis of each odour. It is the reaction of these lost bits that, melting on the mucus layer of the cells, produce the sensation of odour that is flashed to the conscious brain. How these remarkable cells are able to distinguish each and every smell existing on earth is something of a miracle, yet they do! And they can detect infinitely small amounts of scent substances too. Experimentally it has been established that the chemical, ionone, which is a synthetic substitute for the smell of violets, can be smelled by most humans when it is present in a portion of only one part to thirty billion parts of air! Imagine how quickly a wild creature, with a sense of smell infinitely more acute than that of humans, could detect this same chemical in exactly those same proportions! But why do not these smell cells become confused with all of the many odours that surround animals and humans so constantly? Here Creation has installed another one of its remarkably simply safety valves!

Creation provided all the cells needed to detect all the smells and then, realizing the almost-hopeless task she had set for these cells, she made their life simple by constructing them so that they become easily tired. This may be a seemingly-strange way to achieving such an object, but it is one which is most effective, nevertheless. Because the chemoreceptor cells tire so quickly that air carrying a scent which at first seems powerful soon loses its aroma—in a few minutes, in fact—and because this fatigue applies only to the 'smell of the moment,' the nose remains always ready to pick up new smells. This, science now believes, indicates that there is one smell for each kind of chemical that exists in the world.

To man, this ability to tire of one smell while still being able to pick up new ones is of no great consequence just now, for we no longer depend so greatly upon our noses in order to survive. But imagine how handicapped an animal would be without this natural aid! Its nose, often one of the principal factors in its survival, would be absolutely confused by the thousands of smells in the forest: the heady scent of pines; the stink of dead matter; the perfume of wild flowers; the smell of each kind of creature, and of each kind of bird: the aroma of dry earth, and of wet earth; the smell of rain; the smell of water...the list is endless. It would be baffling! Instead, in the same manner in which we quickly become accustomed to, say, the 'stale' smell in a room when we first enter it from the fresh air, animals are able to ignore the smells that normally surround them as they move about in the wilderness, picking them up, keeping them for a minute or two, and then almost literally shutting their noses to them. In this way they can smell a predator quickly, if it is up wind from them—and save their lives.

The smell cells were quickly and instinctively put to work by the young weasel and his brothers and sisters and, when the kits left the den to begin their lives, they carried in their brains the knowledge that would mean life to them in the days and months ahead. They had learned the smell of grouse, of hare, of squirrel, of mouse in the nursery, from the creatures their mother hunted, from the very linings of their nest.

The smell of fresh blood is perhaps the most tempting of all odours to the weasel, for he is especially fond of it. Usually he kills his victims by biting them in one of two favourite places: the base of the skull, or the neck vein, both of which locations yield a quick, strong supply of warm blood, for which he seems insatiable. It is this fondness that makes some people believe that weasels live entirely on blood, which, of course, they do not. In fact, they eat almost anything big enough to kill: mice, shrews, moles, rats, hares, rabbits, frogs, lizards, birds, small snakes, insects, earthworms and many young mammals (if they can catch them when their mothers are not present), such as baby groundhogs. They eat about one-third of their own weight every twenty-four hours and, though adult weasels weigh only between six and twelve ounces, still this is a fair amount of meat to find and kill. Naturally, at times they go hungry for long periods, for hunting is not always good, and then at other times, when their victims are plentiful, they gorge, eating far more than their normal daily ration.

Often, too, a weasel will kill seemingly for the sheer lust of the sport, a thing not unusual in other wild hunters, but this happens but rarely in the wilderness for opportunities of this kind are scarce. Indeed, insofar as this creature's killing sprees have only been observed in man's poultry yards, it may be that, in its natural

FOUR

*This young weasel was five weeks old when found, already it was exhibiting
a great hunger for raw meat, a characteristic of this species.*

home, the little murderer does not indulge in so much slaughter. Chickens penned in a run are there for the taking; big, stupid birds who do not know enough to escape, and cannot anyway! This must be the optimum in temptation to a blood-thirsty weasel! But whether on a killing spree or simply hunting for his needed supper, *Mustela*, for all his small size, is a redoubtable slayer. His slender, supple body, his great strength and his beautiful coordination make him a professional-above-professionals. Though he cannot run fast, he can squeeze his little body into such impossible places as the tunnels of field mice.

In his mouth the weasel carries his main tools of murder, his gleaming, needle-sharp canine teeth. With these and a mind that is agile, of quick wit and super intelligence, he faces life without fear, a small creature of stupendous courage. Often he risks his life because he will not hesitate to attack prey that is twenty and thirty times bigger than he is; which, for those who like comparisons, is akin to a man weighing, say 165 pounds, attacking with his bare hands a creature weighing between 3,300 and 4,950 pounds!

Naturally, life is not just one long round of killing and eating for the weasel. Often he is very busy just keeping his own skin in one piece, and equally often he fails to do this, for he has many enemies. In daytime hawks prey on him; at night owls seek him out. More insidious than these, unseen viruses make him ill and fleas, ticks, roundworms and flatworms weaken him. Though predators like the wolf and lynx and bobcat are not overly fond of his stinky flesh because of his powerful musk glands, these do attack him if no better meal is available.

Breeding time for these savage little fellows is thought to be in early summer, though this is not fully certain and may be subject to variations in climate and the personal feelings of the female weasels. But it is fairly certain that most matings take place between late May and early July and that the gestation time is long, for the young are not born until the following spring, usually in April. This is because, as is the case with some of the other North American mammals, the growth of the embryo is arrested during the winter months. The reason for this is fairly obvious: winters are long and hard, food is scarce and a pregnant mother often needs all the sustenance she can get merely to stay alive. If she were carrying inside of her nine or ten growing embryos that demanded an ever-larger share of her own blood and proteins, mother and babies would not live to see the spring.

From late spring to late autumn the weasel is dressed in its brown coat, but when winter nears it begins to moult. This happens gradually, hair-by-hair, until by snow time the creature is dressed all in white, except for about one inch of black at the tip of its tail, the reason for which I do not know. It may be that Creation puts it there so the weasel's prey are given a sporting chance when being stalked by a killer made nearly invisible against a background of snow. But I do not really think so. Rather I believe that black spot is there for the opposite reason, to help the weasel secure more victims during a time when meat is scarce. It is possible that a potential victim notices this little black spot scurrying over the snow and is fooled into thinking that a shrew, or a mouse, is moving along, thus staying off guard. Who knows!

A weasel barks! Not like a dog, of course, but a sort of bark, nevertheless. It also hisses, and growls, and can scream in rage. And it is one of the most curious (like all of its tribe) of our mammals, often risking death to satisfy itself about something that has caught its fancy. Perhaps this, too, is a necessary part in the life of a small creature that must kill to live, for victims do not come easily. And as a postscript, there are thirty-six different kinds of weasel, not counting its big cousins, the wolverine, the otter, the badger, the skunk and the mink, all of which, improbable as it may seem, belong to this particular tribe of hunters. If these are added to the total, we get forty-one quite distinct kinds, perhaps the most famous of which being the big fisher and his close relative, the pine marten.

STANDING BY THE DEER, the weasel is ready to lope for home, his small belly swollen with the load of meat it now carries. He stands with one dainty forefoot up, his tail resting on the ground, his neck held high and his nose and ears working, for the smell of hare reaches him and, glutton that he is, he is tempted to seek the snowshoe. But that round belly intrudes too uncomfortably upon his latest design, urging him on to his den, instilling an overwhelming desire for replete sleep. So he sets his paw to the ground and moves slowly, regretfully, for there is much meat left on the deer carcass, and that hare is a great temptation. And then he is gone. For a time nothing moves in the area of the decaying remains.

Now a vague greying is noticeable in the sky. It is a long way from dawn yet, but night is waning, and the few stars peeping from between high cumulus are beginning to fade. A breeze is romping through the trees, sighing quietly as it slithers between the needles of the pines, making more lusty sounds as it plucks the few remaining leaves from poplars and birches and oaks. Accompanying this pleasant murmuring, the crackling of breaking ice and the splashing of water tell of a beaver moving upon the lake.

Hopping slowly, with frequent pauses, a big greying hare leaves the shelter of a juniper bush. He is drawn to the deer by the smell of its meat, for although these creatures are mostly herbivorous, they enjoy an occasional meal of protein-rich meat if they can find it, especially in the autumn and during the lean months of winter. This varying hare, or snowshoe hare, or *Lepus americanus*, as it is variously called, has waited in concealment for the weasel to depart, unafraid of the little killer because in a chase he knows he can easily outdistance his enemy. Now, his small nose working, he reaches for meat and with his sharp teeth nibbles off small flakes of the now-cold doe. He munches, his jaws working from side to side in the manner of grass eaters grinding vegetable between flat molars. He swallows and nibbles again and chews again; and repeats the movements five more times. Then, he turns from the meat and seeks grass, eating two or three mouthsfuls before returning to nibble at the meat.

Now a shrew appears and begins eating, a minute glutton who ignores the big hare. But the snowshoe is made nervous by the shrew and although he is safe from attack, he leaves, loping away to find one of his 'forms,' a place where he will rest until hunger again drives him to seek food. The shrew is unperturbed, happy. Soon he, too, is finished and he scampers away and, as his dark shape is lost in the night, there is a scurry in the dry grass and another mouse returns to feed from the wolf kill. And in an instant the mouse dies, for a big grey owl has arrived, his coming unnoticed, for the wings of the owls are silent and there is no moonlight to cast tell-tale shadows. And again the remains of the deer are left alone.

The owl alights in a poplar and soon disposes of his victim. He sits in contemplative silence while the night retreats further and the new day begins to show more clearly, then he launches himself from his perch and glides away, seeking his roost and sleep. Soon the birds of daytime will come and they will harry the big owl if he is caught in the open. And though they cannot hurt him, still their quick dives, the slight impact created by the collision of their smaller bodies against his own, and the few pecks they might inflict upon him, are hated memories of other times when daylight has found him vulnerable to his enemies.

The night and the owl and the meat eaters of darkness have gone and a crisp morning has replaced them. By its light the carcass of the deer shows meagre, and red, and ravaged. The head is still intact, so are the fine legs with their small black hoofs, but the body and haunches are butchered by many teeth. The entrails are missing, and the fawn hair is scattered around the death place and the now maroon blood is dark against the frozen ground. Near the cracked black nostrils, a mound of dead bot maggots offers a rare treat for the two crows that flap down to the kill. Soon the nose bots are gone and the crows scold each other with their hoarse voices as they wrangle over bits of meat. Foolish, greedy birds they are, to waste themselves in argument when there is plenty for both!

Three bright shapes come swiftly to join the crows; blue jays, gorgeous in the fullness of their autumn plumage, fearless and cheeky, positive of their right to share this great meal with the crows, who squawk loudly and make threatening gestures, but are too greedy to attack. The five birds peck at the meat and their voices mingle with the other sounds of day. In a nearby tree, a flock of blackcapped chickadees alight, all a-bustle; chirpy, fluffy little fellows eagerly busy as they scan every nook and cranny in the poplar for insect larvae that are sheltering there. Two immaculate nuthatches flit into a pine, their nasal 'yank...yank' calls ugly in contrast to the well-tailored grey-blue and white of their liveries.

In the lake, a yawning beaver pops his whiskered face out of the water beside his lodge, looks around at his world and decides to duck under again and return to his nest chamber for a long sleep. A few lily pads flop about on the surface of the water, most of them prisoners of the ice, their glossy green now faded to limp yellow. On one of them lies a small, oval, dark brown body that is stippled with little etchings of white. It is a dead water boatman, his paddle-like legs gone, his carcass but an empty husk. A passing jay spots it and swoops low before resuming his flight, his quick

eyes recognizing at once that the beetle is nothing more than a chitinous shell.

Full day has arrived and a pair of pileated woodpeckers steer a course towards the deep woods, their crow-size, chunky bodies paired flashes of black and white, the scarlet on their foreheads fleeting crests of colour as they travel. Below them, strutting chicken-like through a thicket of pines, three ruffed grouse seek leaf buds of poplar shoots that are trying to grow within the dense shadow of the conifers.

The sun yellows the trees and casts clear reflections on the waters of the lake; the frost weakens a little; a few puffy white clouds are trundling slowly in the sky. Morning; autumn morning beside the lake. Peace now for a time, for most of the hunters have been banished to their lairs...

FIVE

AUTUMN HAS GONE and once again I am beside the lake. A minute black speck crawls across an otherwise-empty blue sky and my eyes stray to it. Under my feet and everywhere around me there is snow; deep, powdery snow that conceals the heavy layer of ice that covers the lake's surface. The black dot becomes larger, but it is still formless. The cold bites my ear lobes and I cover them with the woollen flaps of my cap. A downy woodpecker drums daintily on a dead tree. Somewhere in the distance a red squirrel shrills spitefully, perhaps cursing one of his own kind who has intruded in his territory. The moving black shape is larger as it travels across empty sky.

I remain still. The cold invades my nostrils; it freezes the moisture inside my nose each time I draw breath, then retreats before the warm, spent gases that I exhale. It is good here by the lake on this January day. The sun, brilliant in the nooning zenith, highlights the forests with its cheerfulness, warming the mind by its presence, but unable to put much heat into the body, for the temperature has dropped to twenty degrees below zero.

In the sky the black dot has taken shape. It is a raven that flaps lazily in the cold air; a shiny-black scavenging bird who constantly scans the frozen forest seeking carrion for his belly. I search the heavens for another like him, but he is alone, a wanderer from the true north who has migrated here because some unknown whim filled him with wanderlust. He flaps right over my head and sees the movement of my body as I arch my neck for a closer look. The shiny black beak opens and the throat works and he squawks at me. Then he is gone, lost to me over the trees. I am cold. It is time to move on.

This is Saturday and I have thirty-six hours left to me of this place before I must return to the black, mushy snows of the city, and I have a lot of ground yet to cover this day. I move, swinging my right leg, lifting it high so that my snowshoe will clear a small juniper. I tramp down-slope to the lake and set out across it, nine inches of sheet ice and two feet of snow under me.

As I walk, the rapid flutter of small wings sounds sharply close to my head. I stop and begin to slip off my left glove as I raise my eyes and see the rotund, tiny shape of the chickadee. He has landed on a nearby poplar, killed long ago by the beaver of this lake, and he fixes me with one beady black eye as he chirps his impatience. By the time I have removed my glove and reached into my parka pocket for a supply of the crushed peanuts which I now always carry there, four more chickadees have landed in the same tree. Now the ritual begins.

I hold out my hand, opened, upon the palm of which is a supply of broken peanut. The leader of this flock launches himself and lands on my outstretched hand. Daintily, he picks over the nut bits, seeking the best piece, for he is the boss and has earned this right in fair fight with the others. Now he has found a nubbin that is to his liking. He grips it in his black beak and chirps at me, then he flies off to land quickly in another tree.

Now the next in succession to his throne comes to me and repeats the performance. And so all the birds, one at a time, observing strict protocol, until each small bundle of feathers is busy eating peanut, holding his portion with the toe of one dainty foot while he pecks at it, removing minute bits which he swallows.

I remain to watch, and I know that just as soon as one of them has finished his meal he will fly back for more, and again I marvel at these perky little forest gymnasts, so delicate, yet tough enough to dare a Canadian winter. And so friendly, once they learn that man will not hurt them. During the first three years of our acquaintance with this forest, our chickadees tolerated us and accepted the seeds and fat we put out for them; and though they often allowed us to approach them within six feet, always they flitted away if we came too close. Then one day I had the patience to wait outside with some seed upon my outstretched palm and eventually one of them dared to land to get it. That started a practice that is at once alive with trust and, at times, something of a nuisance, for within half a mile of lake or cabin any one of the many small flocks of chickadees that live in my forest will descend upon us and demand food, landing with equal ease on head or shoulder or hand.

There is something undefinably warming in the friendship of these little birds of my wilderness. It has a value beyond par and is almost impossible to describe for those who do not know the touch of something wild upon their flesh. These are not the passive pets of man. They are primordial wildlings uncontaminated by captivity; minute, fragile things that have never known the confinement of a cage and their touch becomes a caress that carries with it the freedom of the wilderness. Wild and free are the birds; wild and free is the human upon whom they bestow their trust.

I watch this flock as it feeds and then continue with my walk. I am facing the north; the sun bursts itself upon the whiteness of the lake's surface, creating dancing little dervish flashes that lance playfully at the eyes. A day of travel over snow such as this, upon a day such as this, will produce snow blindness without the protection of sunglasses. But my eyes are strong and they are accustomed to the sparkle of sun on snow, and I will be exposed to this for only two or three hours.

The frozen lake is quiet now that I have outdistanced the chickadees; no movement disturbs the empty sky, nothing stirs upon the whiteness that lies ahead.

I come to the place where the east and west shores press towards each other and here I see a profusion of tracks highlighted by the sun. This is the runway of snowshoe hares and here, too, come foxes and mink and weasels, for these meat eaters prey upon the humble forest hare.

I notice from the many tracks that mat the snow that the hares this winter are on the increase, and I am glad, for when these creatures become abundant full life comes to the forest. And by the same token, when the hares dwindle, the bushland faces a time of hardship. Two years ago the hares had reached a low point of a regular, mysterious cycle that every nine or ten years produces a feast or a famine in the wilderness.

With unfailing regularity snowshoe hare populations multiply rapidly until they reach a high peak of abundance. Upon their heels come the meat eaters, multiplying of themselves as they feed on the hares, while to the scraps of their meals come other creatures, birds and mice, and squirrels, and insects; and life pulses strong within this region of plenty. There is now more of everything. Body wastes are taken up by the soil, making it richer; trees grow taller, bushes are more abundant; the species thrive, for the living is easy.

Then comes the glut. A high peak is reached and nature must intervene. If last year she was kind and generous, now she is ruthless and cruel. Death is her decree. This is carried out by strange executioners which she had implanted into the bodies of all her creatures. Methodically, the snowshoe hares begin to commit suicide. Entering into a self-induced death trance, one after another the hares perish, the symptoms of their condition and of their final death identically resembling the symptoms of shock.

One day the animals are frisky and well, the next, triggered by some mysterious signal, they begin to go into a decline. Their blood sugar becomes low, they become exhausted; they are seized by convulsions; then they die—of 'natural' causes. Why is this? We know not, and man may never learn why. But we do know how these causes are effected, and now we will again meet our old friends, the adrenal glands, nature's clandestine executioners.

When the brain of an animal signals an alarm to its body, those adrenal glands begin to work hard, with the reactions that I have already described. These series of chemical events are called 'the alarm response' and, if the adrenal glands are allowed to go on working (if the alarm response persists indefinitely, to put it another way) the creature unfortunate enough to be in such a predicament dies of shock, which is a more scientific way of saying that it was literally scared to death. Now, scientists have discovered that it is possible to induce a captured snowshoe hare to

die of shock. By first triggering its alarm responses and then pro-
longing this, laboratory tests showed that the unfortunate creature
died a death exactly similar to that experienced by its no less
unfortunate kindred in the wild.

Of course, these tests showed little that was not already
known, for wild animals and birds suddenly captured often die of
shock. But what prompts the alarm response in large numbers of
hares within one particular forest?

In fact, the alarm response is not outwardly triggered at all,
yet the adrenal glands react as though it *had* been prompted, and
so the mystery deepens and becomes even more complicated.
There is no doubt that the deaths of these creatures are caused by
symptoms exactly similar to those which would be present if the
alarm response was allowed to continue indefinitely. Thus we have
learned something new! We have learned that danger, or the
prospects of instant action, trigger the adrenal glands into boost-
ing the body's defences. But we have also learned that these same
glands can go into slower action, over a period of time, injecting
just enough adrenalin into the body to cause it to 'worry,' to begin
to prepare it for some danger or action that does not appear to
exist. In other words, under certain conditions, the adrenal glands
can trigger a minor false alarm, keeping the creature which they
have alerted in a sluggish but constant state of readiness.

If this happened to a human being (and, of course, it does) a
doctor would diagnose nervous tension and he would prescribe a
sedative which would counteract the effects of the increased
dosage of adrenalin into the system. When it happens to a wild
animal, there is no one there to help and it is frustrated to the
point of death. And that is how nature keeps the population balance among her creatures.

As the numbers of snowshoe hares begin to increase to the
danger point, so the physical and mental stress begins to increase
among the hares (triggered, as I have said, by the action of the
adrenal glands). This is due, we believe, to overcrowding and
stronger competition for food which forces some of the hares into

forest areas where there is less food and shelter and their already high tension begins to climb. Gradually, with the birth of more hares and the decrease of food supplies, the tensions increase and the false alarm response becomes stronger. Towards the end of the winter in the death year, the cold weather, lack of food, the increase among the predators (for when the hares are plentiful, their enemies are also plentiful), plus the nearness of the breeding season putting extra strain on the creatures, causes the adrenal glands to break down. Now the body's normal functions are upset, the blood becomes low in sugar and convulsions seize the unfortunate hares that have become affected. At last death comes, and when it has gone, just enough hares are left to ensure survival for the species.

Every nine years, on an average, come these times of death; and following them, slowly, the species begin to multiply, until again Creation must curb her creatures. Two years ago the hares around my lake had reached a low point, now, it seemed, they were beginning to multiply.

With these thoughts in my mind I move on, only to pause again to examine the track of one hare which leads at an angle across the lake and disappears up the west bank. The track is fresh and this is a good day for indulging a man's whimsy. I decided to follow the hare's pathway, to track the creature to its form, for I knew well the habits of these big hares which seldom move away from their home range, a piece of woodland not more than two acres in area.

Soon I was climbing the shallow bank and here I noted the twin punchmarks of a black squirrel, his route clearly marked as he had struggled with the deep snow. As I looked at these small tracks, the raven I had seen earlier sailed overhead, his voice now a greeting as he flapped away towards the second lake. I watched him go, then turned again and began searching for places that would provide suitable shelter for a resting hare. To my right a clump of skeletal willows offered likely sanctuary, but the tracks did not go to them. Ahead, the tracks merged with others, but,

before utter confusion overtook them, they pointed slightly towards the north where a thick cluster of young, naked alders cast a profusion of black-line shadows on the whiteness of the snow. This place would bear closer inspection. I clumped towards it on my snowshoes, but slowly, stopping often and pretending interest in things other than the alders. Presently I saw the tell-tale black that every hare carries at the tips of his long ears. Six inches beneath this dark area an unwinking black dot was firmly fixed on me and now my eyes could trace the white contours of the hare's body.

I moved nearer slowly, readying my camera for a close-up picture. But the wily hare was on me. A flick of the long ears, a slight sideways glance of the black eye and *Lepus americanus* exploded into long-legged action. I watched him go, running in the familiar semicircle that would take him but a scant seventy-five yards or so from where I stood, and I continued to track him. Four times he exploded from his cover and four times I tracked him. Always we travelled a half-circle at a time, but on the last two wild dashes the hare stopped sooner and broke later. Now was the time for me to talk to him, quietly, soothingly, my words haphazardly-selected and meaningless, my voice monotonously soft. Again this worked. As I slowly neared the hare, I could see the mixture of emotions that gripped him. On the one hand, there was the fear of man driving him to instant action; on the other, an equally intense curiosity in the sound of my voice held him in one place. The long ears swivelled back and forth, scooping up my voice, the powerful haunches were poised, ready for escape. I moved closer yet, then stopped as he set himself for flight with a posture reminiscent of a runner at the line waiting for the starting gun. I spoke more quickly and then I whistled a soft tune. Slowly the haunches relaxed again and the ears turned to capture the sounds I was making.

Now I was close enough for my first picture. I focused the camera and exposed one frame, wound on the film and then advanced another two steps. Thus, intermittently talking and

A snowshoe hare, silhouetted against the trunk of a tree.

whistling and moving a step or two closer after each photograph, I advanced within six feet of the hare. By now he was so accustomed to me and evidently lulled by my voice and whistle that he sat on his haunches and began washing his face. I got the close-up that I wanted and, after a few more moments of talking, I back-tracked, turning now and then to look at him, seeing him settled and obviously unperturbed.

This was not my first such encounter with a snowshoe hare, and it will not be the last, for these hardy, friendly creatures intrigue me, if only because they are so difficult to see in the winter forest. Yet they are so predictable in their escape actions and so equally unpredictable in their dealings with man. In perhaps two meetings out of three they will eventually allow me close to them, but on that third encounter nothing will induce them to stay and I am then forced to abandon the game, for I do not enjoy panicking them.

Each winter at least one of these hares makes his daytime home under our cabin and at dusk comes out to nibble at grain which we set out for him, or to munch placidly on bread crusts. At times they even venture out during daylight and then they can be coaxed near by voice or temptation, greedy for the bread we offer. But do not think that these hares are unwary! Of all the creatures of the northland they are the most hunted, and as a result they are the most cautious and evasive; and that is another reason why they intrigue me so, for they seem able to sense that we mean them no harm.

WINTER IN THE NORTHWOODS is a time of great contrasts. To those unfamiliar with the great primeval forests that stretch across almost one-third of the northern part of the American continent, winter among the evergreens offers harshness and fear and solitude; an eerie silence during its short days; a cold impassiveness during its long nights. During its times of sun, it is a place of blinding white and almost unnoticed green; while during its times of savage storms this vastness of trees and rocks and animal life becomes a terrifying place to the greenhorn, a region to be

A pair of wolves, the male on the left; the black one, a female.

shunned. But those who really know this wilderness quickly learn to love it; and to respect it.

True, the northern wilderness can be harsh, and fearful, and lonely. It can be eerie, and cruel, and pitiless. But it is a place fully, vibrantly alive, a still-uncharted region of limitless adventure that captivates the mind and fires the imagination. In it a man thinks more clearly, and he sees more clearly, and he comes to terms with himself and learns to respect that unexplainable thing which is life. But before a man is ready for this, the wilderness must take him and test him; it must show him its passions, its loves and its hates. And then, if the test has been passed, a creeping newness invades the mind and the eyes see more clearly and values change, and the petty preoccupations of civilization fade before the greatness of a land still untamed.

Out here, walking upon the ice of my lake a thousand adventures are unfolding all around me. Some I can see, or hear; others are beyond my senses, but yet are real. Often I stand, still and silent, and I listen and see and smell this place and I become content. And sometimes I become exhilarated by fear which I cannot escape; and I would not escape it, for it is part of things here and it fines the mind and the instincts.

It was so on the day of the wolves. A small storm was present and fine flakes blew haphazardly about the waving pines as I walked through shallow snow towards the lake. Above the cooing of the wind I heard faint yelps and I stopped, wondering. The hubbub was distant but clear enough to tell me that five or six beasts were clamouring to the north of where I stood. I thought that a pack of dogs was running wild, harassing deer, and I turned for the cabin, seeking my rifle. Dogs that harry game are the worst and most senseless of all the killers. If I could sight on these creatures I would kill them, I resolved.

By the time I reached the cabin, the yelping was louder and coming steadily closer, and I paused only to reach for the .303 and to stuff of box of shells into my pocket. Giving a brief explanation to my wife, I hurried away, loading the rifle as I trotted towards the now clear voices.

Halfway to the lake, the chase turned and headed away from me. I kept going and, as I reached the lake's edge, the creatures turned again and their yelps became again loud. The snow thickened and the wind blew a little harder and the downy white that coated the lake ice was whipped up by wind devils into spirals of rising flakes. It was hard to see through this moving fog, but I fancied I saw quick movement at the northern end of the lake. I took to the ice, keeping close to the east bank and seeking as much cover as I could find, while the creatures that I was hunting came closer.

Then I saw them. Five big, gaunt shapes...timber wolves on the hunt. Instinctively the hackles on the nape of my neck rose stiffly and despite the sweat that soaked my woollen shirt I felt a chill. I knew, of course, that I had nothing to fear. I had a good gun which I could use and I could drop all five of those wolves before they could reach me. But such is the power of indoctrination!

Unconsciously and unbidden, the fearful tales of my childhood tainted my newly-won senses and the superstitions, that undeserved fear in which man has held the wolf for so many centuries, won me over for some moments. Without realizing what I was doing, I slipped a shell into the rifle's breach, then I came-to and accepted this wonderful thing which the wilderness had given me.

I crouched near a stunted poplar and now I used it as a place of concealment from which to watch the wolves. And quickly I learned that they were not hunting. Their cries and their marvellous flashing movements were simple expressions of happy abandon. I watched fascinated.

What a scene it was! Through the swirling snow the five beasts gave me fleeting, quicksilver glimpses as they dashed first this way then that way. Their leader was a big almost-black creature. It seemed that the frenzied game they were playing had for its objective the capture of the big fellow, who repeatedly dodged first one of his pursuers, then another, only to tilt with his shoulder at a third and send it rolling in the snow. And while the mad chase wove an erratic course across the ice, the wolves raised their shrill voices, yelping like dogs, yet not quite like them, for the timbre of the calls was higher, more vibrantly exciting. I had never before heard wolves giving tongue in this manner and had believed until then that they did not bark as dogs do. But here was this pack, playful as puppy dogs, yelping and barking for me, teaching me again that the more I believe I know of the wilderness, the smaller is the sum total of my knowledge.

I know not what alerted the leader of the pack, but suddenly he became immobile, standing stiff-legged and peering intently in my direction. The others instantly stilled their clamour and imitated his stance. In another moment they turned, like well-drilled cavalry, and they sped away, silent now, leaving me spellbound behind my tree.

Curiosity drove me on to the place where they had jousted. The snow was churned, the imprints of their great paws clear in some places, hopelessly misshapen in others and small, melted yellow patches on the snow showed where they had urinated in their excitement. The storm had worsened and, although I had no fear of losing my way in such familiar surroundings, I turned for the cabin, eager to share my new experiences with Joan.

The storm ended shortly after the noon hour and, since Joan needed to buy some things at the store four miles away, we left our property, which we call The Place, and drove to the village of Uphill. An hour later we were back and we must barely have missed my pack of wolves. In our absence they had joyed around the cabin and the dogs among them had urinated copiously against two sacks of coal which I had stacked along one wall. Later that day I heard them again out on the lake and I went to them, taking my camera, instead of my rifle, but this time they heard or smelled me, for there was no storm to mask my progress. They were but dark specks when they fled into the thick forest and I heard them no more during the remainder of that winter.

Late one afternoon in February, I was returning to the cabin after a long tramp through the forest when movement attracted me to the island of the beaver. I was perhaps a quarter of a mile away from it and I was not at first able to interpret the two dark, moving objects that drew my attention. The wind was blowing towards me and, whatever the creatures were, they were so busy with their own affairs that they had not seen me. One was quite small; the other, larger, looked about the right size and shape to be a fox.

I moved off the ice and sought the cover of the stunted trees and shrubs at the lake's edge as I crept closer to the scene, and soon was able to recognize the two creatures. I had been right about the fox. The other was a muskrat. They were engaged in a fierce fight.

Muskrats, though small (not counting their long scaly tails, they measure about sixteen inches in length and weigh between two and three pounds) are of stout heart. With their long, sharp chisel teeth and their strong, agile back legs, they can put up fierce resistance, and the one that was now being attacked by the red fox was defending himself well. The fox, five times the size and weight of the rat, was showing great respect for its intended victim. Each was absorbed in the other and still unaware of my presence.

The fox held his body low and continuously circled the rat. Now and again it slithered in quickly, seeking to get a death-grip on the back of the creature's neck, while the rat constantly swivelled its short, fat body upon its long back legs, always facing the fox. It held its short forelegs pressed tightly against its chest as it stood upright, using its tail for balance. Each time the fox crept close, it jumped into the air and slashed at its attacker with its teeth, all the while emitting a short, shrill cry.

I had no means of knowing how long these two had been cutting and parrying, but the snow was scarred all around them, and I guessed the fight had been going on for some time. Now I was close enough to see both clearly, and I could hear the rat's little squeals as it jumped at the fox, which had evidently come close enough to its prey to receive at least two bites on its muzzle, and these were now bleeding freely.

If I can avoid doing so I do not interfere with the creatures of the wilderness and now I remained still, feeling man's pity for the besieged rat that was so close to providing a meal for the fox, yet fascinated by this primitive battle for survival. I regretted that the light was not good enough for the taking of photographs.

Again and again the fox tried for the death-hold and each time the valiant little rat foiled his enemy's move, attacking constantly, never once giving an inch of ground, and always crying his short bursts of rage. I began to wonder how long these two would keep this up and I found myself speculating on the odds. If the fox was patient enough it must, in the end, defeat the rat, for it was bigger and stronger and of more endurance. And although the rat could inflict some painful punishment on the fox, yet the bites were not dangerously severe, while the fox needed but one opening and it would kill the rat with one bite. Evidently the muskrat had been surprised on its way to or from its den and it had been trapped in the open, unable to scurry down under the ice. Now it could only stand and fight, for there was nowhere to hide from the teeth of the fox.

Suddenly the fox changed his tactics. Instead of making his quick rushes at the rat, he backed off and sat on his haunches, his quick eyes fixed upon the muskrat, his tongue lolling and jerking out of his open mouth, his fangs messages of death for his prey. The rat stood his ground. Raised on his back haunches, his little arms tucked tightly against his chest, he returned the fox's stare, a silent, small statue etched in brown fur against the trampled snow. Each remained immobile and the tactics of the fox were now clear. The rat could not turn to run without quickly being seized and killed, and yet it had so far withstood the fox's direct attacks and had even inflicted some damage on his tormentor. So, the fox resorted to psychological warfare, hoping that the persistent stare and the sight of those gleaming teeth would eventually panic the rat, make it turn and run, and thus offer the fox an easy victory. But that rat would not be panicked.

For almost ten minutes the two remained staring at each other and it was the fox who broke first. Springing to his feet he made a fast rush at the rat, impatience clear in his every move. The rat jumped and squeaked and bit the fox on the nose. The fox backed away, hesitated, and at last turned to leave. He travelled about five yards, stopped and looked back at the rat, who remained on his haunches ready for more trouble, then the fox loped away in obvious disgust. The small rat remained still for another five minutes, then he dropped to all fours and turned in a direction opposite to that which the fox had taken. In another few minutes he had disappeared. This time the fox had lost…perhaps another day the fox would win, and the muskrat would die. This is the way of the wilderness.

I left my place of concealment and headed for home, walking slowly as usual, enjoying this early evening of winter. I was walking towards the west and the setting sun, which had already dropped beyond my range of vision, was still crimsoning the tops of the distant evergreens. Following me was my escort of chickadees, who had again picked up my trail now that I was getting closer to home country and who, one at a time, would importune me, so that I must stop and hand out crushed peanuts. The evening was crisp-cold, the sky clear of cloud and promising a fine array of stars when dark came to backdrop them. There was nothing in me but pure pleasure and contentment, for I was 'at home,' surrounded by old friends: trees which I knew intimately; my small birds; the raucous, more shy blue jays; the inquisitive Canada jays. And I passed the sleeping places of others. Here a fat marmot was asleep under my feet, tightly curled in a hibernating ball; in that gnarled old poplar a raccoon slept; in the dead balsam fir hung the nest of a red squirrel. I knew them all, and they knew me and knowledge breeds understanding and tolerance and respect. In this place a man could die well.

FEBRUARY IS ALMOST SPENT and now the breeding fever has touched many of the animals in my wilderness. The wolves howl their restlessness deep into the night; the raccoons leave their winter dens and roam, lean and love-hungry; the skunks are abroad again, intent on procreating their kind. For a time restlessness seizes the mammals, for the mating craze is strong, a driving force that will not be denied.

Under its skylight of ice and snow the lake water is being churned by the activity of the beavers. Vicious fighting breaks out amongst some of the males, who are not content with the attentions of their life-long spouses and who range under the ice seeking union with strange females. Now the musk glands of both sexes are swollen and show clearly under the skin. Little streams of the strong-smelling liquid they contain are discharged into the water, and in the lodges, and on the 'sign heaps' on the banks of the lake. And although man must guess that the musk is a sex identification guide, and he must guess also that the conical heaps of mud mixed with vegetation that these creatures leave are territorial claim signs, little more is known about both these peculiarities of the beaver. Little, too, is known about the actual mating of wild beaver as this usually takes place under the ice. I have spent many an hour lying prone upon the ice surface (after having brushed the

snow from it), trying to observe some of the rituals of these creatures; in vain so far, though occasionally I have been rewarded by
a glimpse of a blurred, distorted shape as it passed swiftly under
me to become swallowed by the lake. But once, last winter, while
busy with such an experiment, I became the subject of observation for another creature.

I had been lying still for more than ten minutes and the cold
had cut through my heavy clothing and had taken hold of me. It
was time to stand upright and 'double-march' until warmth came
back to me. As I turned to rise, a long, sinuous dark shape started
scuttling away. It was a fisher, and it had been squatting about ten
feet away from me, as curious about my actions as I had been
about the beaver below. It stopped when it reached the east bank,
and it turned and looked me over once more before disappearing
into the forest.

I was pleased to see this big relative of the weasel, for it is a
great killer of porcupines and it had been trapped out of my area
years before and as a result the porcupine population had increased
to the point where they were endangering the forest, girdling tree
after tree as they fed on the bark and tender branchlets.

The fisher, which, when not in a hurry, looks cumbersome as
it moves, is perhaps the fastest hunter of the forest and although it
kills many other small mammals, it has become a specialized
hunter of the porcupine, a creature that is not often attacked by the
larger meat eaters of the wilderness. Daring the quill-encrusted tail
of the porcupine, the fisher can flash into the attack, extend a swift
paw and up-end the porcupine, exposing its soft, quill-free belly.
In a trice the killer bores in, ripping the belly and killing its quarry
and, curiously, if the fisher is careless and gets a few quills stuck
into its flesh, instead of suffering from these, perhaps dying as
other predators do, the porcupine hunter possesses some kind of
secret chemical in its tissues that actually dissolves the barbed
quills. This feat is rivalled only by the wolves (and that poorly),
some of which have been found, healthy and frisky with old quills
embedded in their bodies and even in the lining of their intestines.

Before this day I had seen infrequent signs of fisher around the lake and in the forest. My nearest neighbours, the Adams brothers, who are trappers, had told me of seeing tracks in other areas of the wilderness; but this was the first live fisher I had seen around my lake. I hoped this one would mate, for there were too many porcupines in this area, though the mating time for this animal would not come until April and its young would not be born until eleven months or one year after that, for the fisher is a curious creature.

It is so curious, in fact, that someone, somewhere, away back in the early history of the white man's arrival in North America, became very, very confused about it and named it all wrong! Its name suggests that this large weasel lives on fish, or at least has a great liking for it, but whilst it will eat fish, if someone else takes the trouble of catching it, the fox-sized creature does not fish for a living and it is doubtful that an average fisher ever tastes the stuff during its wild lifetime. Perhaps because it lives in damp areas of

The fisher, a ravenous hunter and an expert at climbing trees.

the forest and because it does not hesitate to swim, the early hunters and trappers decided that it preyed on fish...who knows? At any rate, its Latin name is *Martes pennanti*, which identifies it as a close relative of the pine marten, another member of the weasel family.

On the ground or in the trees the fisher is lightning-quick, and it can even outrun the snowshoe hare, which, in an emergency, can gallop at more than thirty miles an hour and jump distances of twelve feet at a bound. And while the pine marten can flash through the trees with such agility and speed that it has no trouble catching the nimble red squirrel, the fisher has no trouble at all running down and killing the marten, which it does whenever it chances on one of its smaller cousins.

The male fisher measures between three and four feet in length and weighs between eight and eighteen pounds, averaging about twelve pounds, while his mate is much smaller and weighs only half as much as her partner. Once, during the early days of the fur trade, these animals were plentiful throughout North America, from the northland to as far south as Baja, California. But not any more! Their long, silky hair made them too valuable to man for their own good and vast numbers of them were trapped by men of the Hudson's Bay Company and their arch-rivals, the trappers of the North West Company. Irrevocably, the fisher was pushed further and further north and was several times on the brink of extinction, but with the lessening of the 'fur age,' and the settlement of farmlands, its fur was not quite so keenly sought and the creatures began to make a comeback. Today they are still trapped, but because there are fewer of them and because they now inhabit only remote wilderness areas, their future on this earth seems to be assured.

Perhaps at one time the fisher used to migrate south in winter and its time of pregnancy was then normal for a creature its size. Then one year, one of its early ancestors may have been delayed, or prevented by injury, from heading south in the late autumn and nature, ever careful of her creatures, had to change this animal's breeding cycle. If the young of an animal accustomed to whelping in warm weather is born during the cold of a northland winter, the babies will almost certainly perish, so it is possible that natural factors inhibited the growth of that pioneer fisher's babies and delayed the birth. But whatever the explanations, fishers mate in April, a very long carrying period indeed; and that is because the growth of the embryo is stopped at an early stage and does not resume again until months later. The result of this is that fisher mothers must leave their blind, naked babies when these are only about one week old and hurry out to find another mate in order to keep pace with their long carrying time. Usually the female is away from her den for only one night, during these times. But now and then she is gone for longer periods and the young must depend on luck to keep questing predators away from them.

As a rule, fishers remain in a fairly small range, their home territory seldom exceeding six miles and rarely falling below two miles, so the fisher at my lake will probably remain in the area of my wilderness. I hope so, for one of these days perhaps I shall be able to surprise it and photograph it, if I am lucky!

SIX

MARCH ARRIVED QUIETLY, a benign month which seemed to slip in on the heels of a howling February storm. A wicked storm it was, one of those killer-days of intense cold, hard, driven snow and gale winds that sped through the forest in gusts that topped sixty-five miles an hour. Heading into it in our four-wheel-drive car, we had to stop once to pull another motorist out of a snowdrift, and in the few moments that it took for me to fasten a chain on the stranded car, my right ear froze as solid as a board. Fortunately, the condition was brief and the warmth of the car heater soon restored it to normal, but I learned again the old lesson: man dare not underestimate the power of the wilderness.

For two days it seemed that the entire forest was locked in a giant deep freeze. The birds of winter sheltered, the squirrels huddled in their nests, the wilderness was like a dead giant. Then the storm became spent and the sun shone again and a bustling energy quickened the forest. After that it was March. There were no preambles, no fanfares. Yesterday it was February and the land was locked in winter; today it was March and the sun held a new warmth. The barometer rose to above freezing during the hours of sunlight and slowly the stubborn snow began to melt, resisting in those open places where it had drifted into tight banks, lying freely where the land was sheltered by the forest. A song sparrow appeared one morning and trilled his eagerness; the blue jays became more noisy but alternated their lusty squawls with sweet, almost-ridiculous cooings, and male edged up to female and fed her partly-digested titbits from his open beak. The chickadees whistled their deep, three-syllable mating calls and the snow-covered dens of raccoons and skunks and marmots were dug out and small footprints in the snow told their own tales.

Was this spring? Indeed, it was not! This was but a preview, a slackening of deep winter that comes each year to arouse some of

the creatures of the wilderness and send them forth to seek their mates, so that when the real spring comes the birthing of the forest will not be delayed.

Inevitably, though, these mild days with their frost-sharp nights take the mind a leap forward and visions of true spring intrude constantly on the thoughts. At least, it is so with me. Of all the seasons, spring alone can precipitate the mind into full awareness of what is yet to come. On the eve of winter one wonders whether that season will be mild or severe, on the eve of autumn one is not sure enough to forecast its duration; on the eve of summer one must again pose the question: will it be a hot one or a cold one? But on the eve of spring one is sure that the new time of life is just about to begin; one is sure that the trees will bud and leaf, that the birds will mate and rear their young, that the animals of the wilderness, each in its own way, will multiply. Spring is the certain season, while the others can be, and often are, uncertain.

Perhaps it is inevitable that at such times each year I think of the birds that have not yet arrived, but which, I know, are even then beginning their journey from the southlands, obeying the hidden pressures exercised upon their bodies by the increase of daylight. And just as inevitably I repopulate my lake with their various species, and I see them again in mind's eye, and I wonder if I shall be lucky enough to get certain pictures of species. But this year, my thoughts have turned from those photographs to a new path and, last Sunday, as I returned to our cabin from my lake and I heard the trill of our first song sparrow of the season, I set back the clock of time.

I went on a journey into the past. A long journey through lost ages to a remote and terrifying time when huge, cumbersome creatures lumbered over the earth and strange, crow-sized birds flew weakly in the skies. I returned to the Mesozoic Era to dally in the Jurassic Period of 165 million years ago, there to find the Archaeopteryx who was to the birds what Adam was to man.

By now, North America's land mass was fairly well developed, though shallow seas still dominated along our west coast; primitive plants, particularly the dicots, forerunners of many of today's flowers and plants, flourished in open places, while giant conifers had become common and cast their shades over strange grasses.

Through some unfathomable mystery of creation the Archaeopteryx had developed, spawned by the sea, sired by an unknown reptile. How? Why? It is doubtful that we shall ever have the answers to these questions, but this half-bird, half-reptile was born; there is no doubt, for its fossil outline has been preserved in the rocks that existed in its day.

This first bird had teeth and a long, lizard-like tail upon which it grew primitive feathers; its wings had the first three fingers free and these were equipped with efficient claws that almost certainly helped the creature climb about its tree dwellings. Its legs and feet were bird-like, adapted for perching on tree branches, but on these its reptilian ancestry showed more strongly, for definite scales clothed them. Though its wings grew long flight feathers, scientists now believe that this bird was a weak flyer (the three fingers with their claws suggest this) and that it lived on insects. Of course, much of this is conjecture based on the evidence of a few fossils, but to support this, creation has linked that early bird of prehistory with another that still lives in this century, the Hoatzin of British Guiana (Guyana). As a chick, it spends its life climbing about its nesting tree, its wings being also equipped with fingers and claws, its tail a miniature replica of its remote ancestor and, when only a few days old, endowed with another reptilian trait, the ability to dive and swim through water with perfect ease.

Thus, millions of years ago, birds, like mammals, evolved from reptiles, and slowly developed, losing their teeth, their reptilian tails and most of their scales—but not all of them, for even the barnyard fowl retains scales on its legs and feet—replacing these with feathers of many hues. And although we tend to look on these soft, colourful things as delicate and beautiful, yet they are eminently practical, and they are strong, and elastic; efficient, yet simple coatings which are, nevertheless, wonderfully designed.

Feathers begin life in a follicle, or pit, in the skin of the bird and grow much like the hair of mammals except that they have their own blood supply, and they are protected by a tough sheath of keratin, the substance that also forms the claws of mammals and the fingernails of man. Through an opening at the beginning of the feather's shaft, blood flows in to nourish a rate of growth which can attain a quarter of an inch or more each day, until the feather becomes mature, the blood-opening becomes closed and the feather dies. By having died, it does not become useless. On the contrary, it is now that its real assistance to flight begins and, if such a feather be lost through accident, or during the bird's moult, a new, live one replaces it and the process begins again.

It hardly need be said that when Creation made feathers, it built the perfect medium with which to clothe creatures that fly under their own power. Feathers are light, yet they offer wonderful insulation against the cold and heat, and yet they are strong enough to beat the wind and carry their owners through high winds or storms. Those on the body of the bird provide covering; those on the wings and tail, while also offering some body-protection, are its instruments of flight. All of them are intricately designed so that each of the many thousands of filaments that make up one feather locks together by means of little microscopic hooks, rather like zip-fasteners. When a bird beats its wings in flight, the primary feathers come together in a curved, smooth surface during the downward stroke, and come apart, like spread fingers, on the upward stroke, offering resistance to the air when the bird brings its wings down and no resistance when it lifts its wings up for a new stroke. To further help the bird to fly (and to stay in the air), its bones are hollow, and therefore light, and its breast bone or keel, has developed powerful muscles that pump the wings and, because of their weight, also help it to stay 'on an even keel.'

Naturally, flying is a tiring, strength-consuming business and the muscles that do all the work need a constant supply of food: blood. To keep this blood flowing through the muscles, the heart of a bird beats very fast, and therefore pushes the blood rapidly through the veins to the muscles, and then returns it to the lungs from whence it came. Now, to replenish this used blood, the bird's lungs need lots of oxygen and nature has taken care of that, too, by placing inside the bird's body several air sacks, which carry a reserve air supply and, incidentally, help cool the bird. But even so, the bird's temperature is higher than that of most mammals, ranging as high as 112 degrees Fahrenheit in some species, while its heart can beat as fast as ten times a second. And if you don't think this is fast, try counting to ten within the space of one second!

Because birds have no sweat glands, they have learned to lose heat by opening their beaks and vibrating the walls of their throats when their air sacks cannot keep pace with the day's heat. During the summer, especially when they are raising their young, they must do this often, for not only do they themselves require vast quantities of food, they must also feed their voracious babies which, small as most of them are, can pack away amazing quantities of insects, seeds or green foods. No wonder that a bird's heart needs four compartments (man's has only two) in order to keep up with the to-and-fro dashing that its owner must do merely to eat enough to live on. That is why I never cease to be amazed by our chickadees during winter time, for, tiny mites that they are, they must be constantly eating and constantly burning up energy in a never-ending race with death. And when winter is severe and food supplies are scarce, few of them should survive to see the spring; yet they do! With a tenacity and strength incredible in such small creatures, they flit back and forth through the forest, forever foraging, finding a morsel here, another there, eating, eating, eating, or they will die frozen on their night perches.

When times are good, though, they do not always eat all that they find, even in winter. Around my lake and my cabin, where there is always a good supply of feed for them, they often fly into a nearby tree with a bit of peanut and hide it in some nook on a branch, after which they immediately fly back to me and demand more, peeping indignantly if I am not quick enough for them. And it was their cheeky voices that intruded into my thoughts of prehistory and returned me to the reality of March in the northland.

That year March became a capricious month. Early in its life it brought high temperatures and soft winds and days of pure, warm sunshine, and then, during its second week, it frowned and unleashed upon the wilderness a fury as savage as that of dead February. It was a Friday afternoon; and it had been a pleasant morning. Out of nowhere, a vicious west wind came to life and brought fine snow with which to obscure the light. And the temperature dropped thirty degrees and now winter was back; stark, cold, cruel, inevitable winter. The sap of the trees and plants, which had been coaxed upwards from its shelter in the root systems, retreated hurriedly; the love-making of the jays ceases; the chickadees moved faster as they sought their food; the raccoons returned to their burrows; the tracks of the hares faded from the forest floor.

The storm spent itself during the night, but the cold remained and again the forest reflected the mood of caution that winter forces upon all who live in the northern wilderness. In the morning I prepared to go for a walk, selecting camera and lenses and a fresh supply of peanuts for the chickadees. As I was leaving, Joan warned me against going without snowshoes, for there was a crust on the deep snow and it would not hold my weight. But I was stale; I wanted exercise. That had been a slow winter for my body, a winter of sitting at the typewriter in the city and of little physical activity in the wilderness, for I had been busy photographing birds and small animals around the cabin. So I left the snowshoes behind.

A quarter of a mile from the cabin I debated returning for them, then decided that my body needed some punishment for its laziness. And punishment it received! The easiest way to describe that four-mile tramp is to liken it to a journey up a steep staircase that is four miles long! But that hardly does justice to the stubborn treachery of March snow; deep snow, it is, and it has become crusted in layers of ice, like the frosting on a tiered cake. Sometimes these ice-layers will hold a man's weight, and at other times they will not, and the feet break through; and then a man finds himself almost waist deep in snow. And after a time, each step becomes a lottery. Will the crust hold? Will it give way? In any event the weight must be controlled, the body balanced, delicate equipment held out of harm's way in readiness for a fall.

After an hour of this punishment, I was bathed in sweat and my heavy parka was fastened to my belt, a bulky cushion that slammed against my legs as I walked. Half an hour after that, my insulated vest came off and my sleeves were rolled up and my shirt was unbuttoned to my belt. And still I perspired as I tramped over and through that snow; and yet the temperature was down to three degrees below zero! Now and then I stopped to take photographs and now the snow helped, for it provided a smooth, firm surface for my tripod. But it was mostly still-life that I photographed that morning, for my progress was too noisy and the creatures of the wilderness kept out of my way.

"You look like you're coming back from a war," was Joan's greeting to me when she saw me as I returned to the cabin.

I suppose I did, and perhaps, in a sense, I was returning from war, but one far different to that which she alluded. Out there I had fought one more fight, and won it, with the help of the wilderness; I had come to grips with the frustrations and concerns of city living, and I had ousted them. Gone now were the muscle tensions caused by high speeds on packed highways that take hold of the shoulders, and the neck, and keep them in a rigid stance; gone was the foulness from deep down in the lungs; the stiffness of the joints, the fretful nerves. Once more clean air was inhaled deeply into the lungs, the shoulders moved loosely, the joints responded more fluidly, the nerves rested. I was bathed in sweat, my face was slightly browned from the glare of sun on ice, but I was replenished already. And I had yet one more day here to further prepare me for another week of 'civilized' living in the bustle of a ravenous metropolis. Man must live in cities, for this has become his way; and the demands of modern living force us all to strain into the yoke of urban life, but in all of us there still lingers a desire for freedom which has been inherent in all living creatures since the dawn of life on earth. In some it is buried deep, expressing itself now and then in strange, distorted ways; in others it is stronger, and yet it is unclear, and it is these others it drives deeper into the clutches of urbanity in an effort to appease its power. A few it drives to action of another sort. It sends them across rivers, and up mountains; it places them on ships and trains and aircraft and it sends them into strange lands, seeking. And of these only a few really find. I am one of these. I have discovered freedom out here in my wilderness. But my search was long, and misguided often, and it took me to three continents and to a score of countries. And in the end my discovery was accidental, and I still ask myself: Did I discover the wilderness, or did the wilderness discover me? As yet I cannot answer that question.

ONE MORNING in mid-March, Joan drew my attention to a lean, long groundhog that was trotting past the cabin on snow that was now crusted hard. He was our neighbour from last year, the only groundhog I have known to climb a steep pole and sit on a window feeder eating grain, which he used to do twice a day during the summer. Now he was fresh out of his winter's sleep and had dug his way free of the snow that plugged his hole, which was located just behind our outhouse. The fat of summer and autumn living had been 'burned' off during his sleep and now he was looking for a mate, wandering around the area hoping to find a female. But he was early! His was the only hole uncovered until then in the immediate vicinity of the cabin and, although these creatures range some distance during the mating urge, they do not travel too far from their dens, for they are so slow that even a man can run them down. In fact, the only time that they travel more than a couple of hundred yards from their den is during the spring mating time.

Sight of this fellow sent me in search of my camera and parka and put me on route to the lake. There are several of his kind denning near the south-west end of it and I wondered if they also had emerged from underground.

It was a perfect day for a walk. Whereas the week before I had continuously broken through the snow crust, now the snow was as hard as a highway and walking was better than in summer, for all the underbrush was tidily imprisoned under the crusted white. And because there was about half an inch of fine snow dusted over the crust, the creatures of my wilderness had left me a clear record of their doings during last night and this morning.

It fascinates me to note the importance which a body of water has for the creatures of the forest, and at no time of year can this be better observed than during a day such as I have described. Half a mile from the lake the tracks of hare and squirrel and fox and deer and wolf, to name but a few, ran in all directions, and there was distance between each cluster of imprints. In places, fox tracks were superimposed on hare tracks which the predator had been hunting, while the tiny pug marks of squirrel crossed both sets. Between these marks, perhaps, a deer had walked. The tracks were numerous, but they fanned in all directions. But as I got closer to the lake, the tracks came closer together so that presently they converged on to various ancient game trails. It was as though each creature had started from the lake to fan out into the bush, although during this season, when the ice conceals the water, the lake has no particular attraction to creatures such as the hare. However, because of the lush growth on its banks where food is plentiful and, if the snowshoes are not in one of their periodic declines, numbers of them make their homes in the area. This, of course, draws predators to the scene and many of these, being quite migratory by nature, such as the coyote and timber wolf, invariably check the frozen lake and its banks in the hopes of an easy meal. Deer, likewise, often cross the ice when the less severe weather of March draws them out of the areas of dense shelter in which they have spent the thick of the winter.

Also, because food is plentiful around water, squirrels and groundhogs live in large numbers in the neighbourhood, while, of course, creatures such as the muskrat and the beaver must live there or perish. For good measure, and because small killers like to live

Timber wolf stalking a deer

as close to their prey as possible, weasels and mink can always be found near water, summer and winter. Thus, to discover the kind and quantity of creatures that live within a particular forest, a naturalist need but visit the lakes or rivers that are to be found in it to compile his list. And winter is an excellent time in which to identify those creatures that do not hibernate or abandon an area during the cold.

My lake is no exception. Around it and under it all manner of creatures dwell and the dens of many of these are known to me. At this time of the year, when new vitality begins to take hold of the wilderness, and when the movement of birds and animals is written plainly upon the snow, I set out to take stock; to determine the kinds and numbers of creatures that inhabit the area around the lake and to try to find out if some of last year's hibernating animals have survived the winter and their enemies. This can be a sad task for a human who has allowed his rational sentiments to become too involved with the wild things of a northern forest, for life is short here and two or three seasons is, on an average, all that a wild creature can hope for.

In human terms such a life is very short. But time is of no consequence to the animals of a forest, which live for the day, patiently and stoically accepting that which comes to them, be it feast or famine, life or death. And it is this that makes the wilderness so vibrant, for always its creatures reflect the inbred capacities that allow them to live vitally, to burst their beings upon each new day without the inhibitions of civilization. From the smallest insect to the largest bear or wolf these beings of the wilderness have no concern for the clocks of man. Instead their lives are regulated by their own built-in clocks, instruments of variety and intense mystery which, though we know that they exist, we have not been able to locate or even to understand beyond a vague way.

That man, too, once owned his share of these clocks there is no doubt, for a few still linger in our beings, perhaps the best known of which is the one which, in some of us, can be called upon to act as a morning alarm if it is 'set' before going to sleep by repeating quietly to ourselves: "I will wake at such-and-such an hour." My own works well, if I summon it hard enough, but to the best of my knowledge this is the only one left in my body still capable of function.

In animals, especially wild ones, the opposite is true; their clocks function with precision. And plants and insects are also furnished with these 'time-pieces.' The honey bee, for example, can 'tell the time,' even though it may be in the pitch-dark of its hive, having the ability to know exactly how many hours have passed since it last saw the sun. Ants likewise can tell time, as can plants, and insects; so can birds, and many of these creatures and plants know with enviable exactitude when to do certain things. But in addition to these instinctive 'clocks,' things have other finely-tuned 'instruments' that can perform what seem to be veritable miracles. The bluebottle fly, for instance, has four nerve cells in the joints which connect its antennae to its head that are effective speedometers, or wind speed indicators. These become activated when the antennae are bent back to the fly's speed and seem able to signal flight instructions to the insect's brain. The further back that the antennae are bent by wind pressure, the more slowly does the creature fly and, conversely, if it has need of extra speed, the faster it flies.

In similar manner, toads have a built-in 'homing' device which allows them to return each spring to their birthplace, each amphibian following his own course through forest and brush which, to a creature of that size, must present enormous obstacles. Yet, day or night, sunshine or cloud, the toads unerringly chart their courses through the giant labyrinths of nature. And then, if weather conditions have caused their birth pools to dry, or if man has bulldozed them aside, these small wild things, so tenacious in their navigation, will not spawn anywhere else, though other pools may be within sight of them. Having made their incredible journey and found their water supply no longer there, instinct forbids them from spawning anywhere else. They die unfulfilled.

Yet another mystery surrounds a wasp with an impossible name: the Ichneumon wasp, which feeds upon certain wood-boring insects. The females of some members of this family have a tiny drill projecting from their stomachs, which they use to make a hole in order to reach the larva of the horntail fly. Connected to this drill is the ovipositor, or egg-laying tube and, once the wasp has made its hole, it deposits an egg on the horntail larva. Now, one may wonder, how does this insect know exactly where its prey is located under the bark of the tree? Outwardly there are no signs of the horntail. Though it is theoretically possible that the wasp can hear the fly larva, this theory tends to be ruled out because some of the wasp species will only lay their eggs on one or two specific fly species. In these cases at least, sound can be ruled out. Often I have watched these insects and the more I see of them the more they astound me. A female wasp will dash up and down a branch or trunk, obviously seeking some sign meaningful only to herself; suddenly she will stop, press down her abdomen and begin to drill. A moment or two later she flies away and on each occasion that I have taken the time and trouble to dig around the spot, I have found a horntail larva, the wasp egg snugly laid upon it. How the wasp does it I do not know and, as far as I am aware, neither does anybody else.

The ways of Creation are countless and many of the mysteries that these pose are impenetrable. But yet there is much that a patient, careful person can learn of the wilderness; all that is needed is time…and that is one commodity that I am jealous of these days. Daily I regret the many hours that I once frittered away in idleness, for no matter how hard and for how many hours I may now devote myself to the study of nature, I will never be able to make up my lost time. Still I am content now, for each weekend takes me to my lake and my forest and each weekend adds a little to my store of knowledge. I feel that I am doing all that I can do to increase this knowledge and to share it with others, and more than that man cannot hope to do.

Of course, some of the things that I am now 'discovering' for myself have already been discovered by many others. But to me they are new and perhaps on occasion I may notice just a little more than the last man and thus knowledge grows, if it is recorded. It was thus with our raccoons a few years ago, creatures which, all the literature says, are extremely fond of water and always wash their food in it. I had read this many times and their Latin name, *Lotor*, means 'the washer.' But after a lasting and close friendship with no less than fourteen wild raccoons, of whom only one evidenced any special liking for water, I must doubt the fullness of this creature's love of the substance.

Naturally, they drink it and, just as naturally, because they eat "anything" upon which they can get their capable hands, they frequent streams and lakes, where frogs, tadpoles, leeches, mussels and small fish can be had for the taking. But away from the water they are equally ready to eat grass, or insects, or carrion, or almost anything else, without displaying any concern for their supposed favourite element. In fact, of the five raccoons that we raised until they were able to fend for themselves, only one showed an actual preference for water. The others used it on occasion, but were glad to be rid of it after ten or fifteen minutes of play and they could

A young raccoon, one of the more inquisitive inhabitants,
often frequenting streams and lakes.

not be induced to behave as raccoons are supposed to when eating. If we gave them some food, they would take it away from the water tub we keep for them and consume it on *terra firma*, only playing with it in the bath if they were not hungry.

I am fairly well convinced that the raccoon's insatiable curiosity and the extreme sensitivity of his fingers have given rise to the belief that he dunks *everything* in water and that he could not live without it. Undoubtedly, what a raccoon sees he generally likes to feel and he (or she) will spend considerable time just plain *feeling*, be it water, or food, or stones, or just his own fingers. If he should happen to be near water, sated from plenty of food, and has just captured a wriggly crayfish, why he will almost certainly dunk it and feel it. But he will eat it quickly enough without the water.

During the summer we keep a large aluminum tub under the eaves to catch the rain water, and it is generally full. In it I place a large stone, for it is the drinking place of many of our creatures and we offer them a way out for those times when they slip off the edges and fall into it. The raccoons come to our cabin every night and, when we are up there, they enter our home through door or window and enjoy the foodstuffs we give them. Only one of the twelve to fourteen coons that visit us takes his food over to the water tub; the rest eat on the spot and only go to the water for a quick drink before walking off into the night in search of mischief. But, in case any reader should misunderstand me, let me say that I am not denying that raccoons like water and make use of it and even wash their food in it. What I am saying is that they are not as concerned with it as the literature would have us believe. Which is another way of saying that man should never try and generalize about the creatures of the wilderness.

Another interesting observation that I made a few years ago was when I noticed that hares, while primarily vegetarians, are also carnivorous if they get a chance. So are squirrels, and chipmunks, and, in fact, most (if not all) of the small 'grass eaters,' of the wilderness. Naturally, many other people have observed this also, but until that time I was like the vast majority of my fellows, convinced that a grass eater only eats grass and that a meat eater only eats meat, both of which general suppositions being incorrect, for the hunters are just as likely to eat grass as are the hunted. Which brings me to another observation, again common knowledge among biologists and naturalists, but which, until that time, was new to me. This concerns the position of the eyes of wild creatures, and although I have just warned against generalizing, in this case I do not hesitate to do so, for what I am about to relate concerns the physical of creatures, not the habitual.

After a few years of watching and studying wildlife, I was out walking one afternoon when I startled a hare and the position of its eyes on each side of its head made me realize that its range of vision was much wider than my own. And there is reason in this, the reason of Creation, for those that do the hunting must have eyes in the front, for two eyes that can focus on one object are needed to judge a killing jump. And the creatures that are hunted must have eyes on the sides, for they must be able to see all around, each eye acting independently of the other. And similarly, Creation has placed the ears of the creatures; those of the hunted able to swivel in many directions, shaped for capturing the slightest sound coming from behind, or in front, or from the sides; and those of the hunters having less movement, and being shorter, are able to concentrate more fully to the front, where the need for hearing is greatest.

In like manner, I learned that movement spells caution to the hunted and interest in the hunter, while immobility often goes undetected by both, if scent does not enter the nostrils of the creatures. Often I have used this in order to watch animals and birds upwind of where I was sitting or standing. And I learned, too, that amongst some of the wild things of the wilderness, casual passage through the forest is less likely to startle them than stealthy, 'hunting' movement. Well I remember one morning in autumn during the hunting season, when deer were being hunted in my area; I was out with my camera and had stopped to look at an abandoned bird's nest in an old stump. I was staring absently, relaxed and unmoving, when a doe deer stepped quietly out of the underbrush, looking often over her shoulder towards the direction from which she had come. She was heading straight for me and I remained still and she passed by me, only some yards from where I was standing. Then she stopped, about twenty feet from me and she turned and examined me, openly curious and undecided, perhaps scenting me, or noticing the slight heaving of my chest. For the space of half a minute she looked me over and then, quite casually, she turned and stepped away with that springy, graceful stride of the white tail deer. But these are thoughts of spring, and summer, and autumn; the thoughts of March should be different, for during that month it is yet cold, and the nights are still short, and silent...

A night of March in a snow-crusted forest can be a strange, haunting experience. I remember one such recently. Darkness had brought renewed frost and I had been restless inside the cabin and, because the moon was full and the sky clear of cloud, I decided to walk my restlessness away.

The snow was hard, a wide, broad pathway to anywhere and, although I had not consciously chosen a route, my steps turned towards the east and the lake. It was a lovely night. The evergreens were warm dark cones against the moonlit sky, the poplars and maples trellises stood with bare, still branches; the quiet so intense that the scrunch of my boots upon the snow was a harsh sound that caused me to pause often and kept me standing still each time, loath to break again the silence. Once I turned to look at the cabin, a rectangular silhouette against the whiteness, the one window which I could see glowing with the yellow light of gas.

Afterwards I hurried towards the east, suddenly anxious to reach the lake and stand beside it quietly while the night grew older and my mind wandered aimlessly in unaccustomed release. I walked steadily now, uncaring of the noise that I was making, and twice snowshoe hares dashed away from my path to run their short, half-circles and stop, rigid with tension, until I had passed them by a safe margin. The frost was attacking some of the damaged trees of the forest. Now and then sharp, staccato reports echoed through the wilderness, loud testimony to the strength of water which, harmless during the hours of sun, now swelled its bulk as it turned to ice, causing the tissue of the tree to split suddenly, protesting with its short bark. Even granite rock becomes the victim of water at these times.

I reached the shallow valley that leads to the lake and here I was in the country of maples and poplars and hazels, the range of the hare and the grouse, the pathway of the deer and of their hunters, the timber wolves. The moon cast long shadows on the white snow, the trees whispered quietly, managing with only a few of last year's sere leaves to make a subdued murmur on this quiet night. I stopped amongst the trees and the quick-moving, shadowy outline of a flying squirrel intruded fleetingly on my vision. For an instant I saw him as he glided to a large poplar, his 'wing' membranes taut, his legs spread wide, his small, bushy tail trailing like a rudder; then he was gone and never a sound did he make as he landed and scurried up the tree.

At last I was beside the frozen lake. Before me I could see the ragged outline of the main beaver house that huddles on the small island in the centre of the water. Towering behind this were the three giant pines that I use as a landmark when wishing to move directly to the beaver dam. This time I had not used them and I had come out higher than the dam, more to the north of it. I changed course, for I wanted to cross over its lip and stand on the far side of the lake. The ice now was treacherous; I could not trust it any more this year and I must, from now until the next big cold, walk longer distances to cross to the east bank.

On that night I only got halfway across the lip. The sound of water rushing out of the lake through two below-ice spillways turned me from my purpose and, as often happens to me when I am out walking through the wild, my original object was abandoned for this new interest. What halted me was not the sound of the water, for this runs year-round in lesser or greater quantities according to the beaver engineers, but memory of an incident that had occurred years earlier, when I had been crossing a frozen stream on a tractor and the ice had broken, dumping me into icy water. At the time I was, not unnaturally, too concerned with removing my person and tractor from the water to stop to wonder at the reason for my ducking, but yet I subconsciously noted that the ice was about nine inches thick and that there was an air space a full two feet in depth between the underside of the ice and the water.

Downstream from this place the beaver had damned the creek and, after I was dry and warm again and the tractor was salvaged, I began to be interested in that air space. Was it there by design or by accident? I leaned towards the design theory. It seemed logical that beaver, intelligent enough to construct incredibly-strong, intricately designed dams, should possess enough wit to allow a thick cover of ice to form over their waterways, and then release enough water to create an air space. Thus they were allowed to swim above water instead of under it, protected from the weather and their enemies, and able to intake as much air as they needed.

Well, it was only the beginning of a theory, but it lingered in my mind and during other winters in other places I tested it and in each case I found that, where conditions of flow permitted, there was always an air space between water and ice.

Standing on the lip of the dam that night it occurred to me that I had not cut through this ice to test my belief and, with my belt-knife, I laboriously hacked a hole in the ice some distance from the dam. On this lake at that time and that year the ice crust was four and one half inches thick. Beneath was an air space not quite two feet in depth. I have not, of course, *proved* my theory, for such proof requires stronger, scientific evidence, but I believe that my deductions are distinctly probable. The beaver is nobody's fool. It is reasonable to grant him enough intelligence to make himself as comfortable as possible and, though I have found no mention of this trait in any of the literature that I have studied, this does not mean that the trait does not exist. After all, very little is known about the habits of free beaver during wintertime, for their study on such occasions would require long submersions under ice water by a man equipped with aqua lung and diving suit. It is then likely that his presence and the rush of waste bubbles in the water would disturb the normal life of the winter lake. Perhaps one day I may dare to go down, but with a long rubber tube instead of an aqua lung, which will allow me to breathe and exhale through it and thus not disturb the water. But that's a tough assignment and I may never undertake it.

SEVEN

IT IS MORNING in April. The sun has cleared the trees; it seems to sit above them radiating molten yellow against a pale blue heaven that is flecked with shreds of distant cloudlets. Solid rays of sun shatter the surface of the lake, to burst away from it again as thin shafts of reflection that cause the broken ice and open water to glisten with the sheen of fine jewels. The temperature is forty degrees, the day promises to be warm by northern standards.

In the water a quiet beaver moves, heading north. Around the lake the trees have become fresh, the evergreens painted a new shade, the maples and poplars and birches, and the hazels and alders and the shrubs showing their hues of yellow and scarlet and light green, for the sap has risen from the roots and is now flooding through the veins of each species, adding for a short time almost autumnal colours to this scene. Not too many days before this time, relative silence dominated this area. Today, the ebullient song of birds fills the air with the earliest of all music. In the reed beds, where the water is open, can be seen the dark tones of the ducks, the mallards and black ducks, and the pintails and wood ducks. Now and then the cra-aagh of a great blue heron which is slowly, woodenly pacing the west bank, searching for frogs. Of course, the blue jays must be here with their lusty, throaty screams of delight as they flit from bush to tree and back to bush again while the red-winged blackbirds fill a dead pine that stands at water's edge, their dark bodies giant punctuation marks against the sky, now and then the flash of yellow and blood red, identifying the males amongst them.

Holding a noisy conference in a tall pine a quarter of a mile distant, is a flock of nineteen crows, its cacophony harsh but impelling. The shiny black bodies of the birds seem in perpetual motion as they hop from branch to branch or as they majestically

pace along a perch, all the while pumping their bass cries to the accompaniment of their working beaks. In contrast, the sweet tones of the white-throated sparrows, flute-like voices of five syllables which say clearly: Poo-oor Sam Peabody-Peabody-Peabody.

High in the sky, courting hawks wheel and dive and soar with the incomparable grace of the hunting bird, stocky creatures of the air now concerned with the annual ritual that demands of the male a show of aerobatics in which his spouse must eventually join. So the two presently dip and climb and glide in unison, at times speeding side by side, at other times crossing in swift glide; as quickly splitting to climb high into the sky and then plummet their bodies towards earth in streaking dives. Tomorrow or the next day these hawks will turn their aerial talents to the hunt; today they court, though they have been mated for a number of seasons; and the small, helpless beings upon which they prey fear not their shadowy bodies, for the forest knows that this is not their time to kill.

Near the lake, invisible in the forest, a ruffed grouse cock drums his call, at once both a tattoo of love and a battlecry to rival males. Bup-bup-bup-bupbupbupbuprrr, the rhythm is loud, strong; it vibrates in the air and is quickly answered by another bird, some distance away. The two beat their tempos, each preoccupied with a hen, each content to ignore the other provided he remains in his own territory.

In the trees bordering the lake, but away from its edge, red squirrels are trilling their spite-filled warning to their kind. Each is staking out his territory, for these small gymnasts have mated, and male and female are now enemies and must claim their one or two acres in which to feed and live and garner the provisions for the next winter's survival. Now and then, one of them will skitter halfway up the trunk of a young sugar maple and will nip at the bark. From the wound in the tree's skin, sweet sap flows and the squirrel laps quickly of the fluid that is high in glucose and is needed to replenish his body after the spartan diet of winter.

Overhead, silhouetted against the sun and sky, a flock of Canada geese rides the airways on its way northward, the V of the

A great blue heron by the edge of the lake, ever alert for frogs.

Perched by its nest, high in the branches the great blue heron keeps watch.

formation undulating slightly. A few stragglers race to find places in the rear, their haunting cries ghostly sounds that reach faintly to the earth and water of the forest. This flock will not land here today, but perhaps tomorrow another will come and it will touch down amidst the great, noisy honking and gaggling and the crash of heavy bodies splashing into the water. And a few will linger here and raise their young, and will stay on this lake and on the others around, until autumn calls to them again and they must rise to join a new formation that is migrating to the southlands.

The croaking of a frog is clear. But it is silenced quickly. The heron has eaten. One frog will not spawn later this month. The heron calls and his mate answers. She is concealed by last year's bullrushes and she, too, has eaten already this morning and is stilting along seeking more prey. A thin muskrat takes fear and slides into the water, swimming quickly beneath it to find another place in which to feed. It is unlikely that the bird with the spear beak will attack the rat, but he has not wintered well, for he is one of last year's young that could not find a good den last autumn and has had to spend his winter in the discomfort of a shallow bank dwelling, open to the cold and often fleeing in panic from the gleaming fangs of a hunting mink. But he survived. And now it is spring and there is new growth on which to feed and grow strong, and this is enough and the rat has less concern. Still, he is cautious, and this is good, for thus he will be more likely to survive through the dangers of the year that lies ahead.

Galloping daintily along a thin runway through the dead grass, a white-footed mouse is seeking a mate. Already this morning he has fought a rival and one of his ears has been gashed, but so thin is its tissue and so ill-equipped is it with blood vessels that only twin edges of brown show in the lips of the new wound. He stops at a likely place. He has found a female ready to accept him. He sings his small, reedy song for a moment and then the two become locked in the breeding ritual.

Several miles away from this scene, but yet linked closely to the lake and its creatures, a timber wolf-bitch is preparing the den in which she will birth this year's young. Outside its entrance, a dark-grey shape against the freshly-dug brown earth, the male lies, resting, a great dog that is at peace with the forest, content now to let his mate fuss with the nursery that will be forbidden to him for several weeks after the pups are born. During that time he will be forever busy, hunting alone, ferrying back meat for his mate, carrying it at times in his mouth, at other times swallowing it and then regurgitating it outside the entrance of her den.

In holes in the ground all over the forest, the groundhog females are also preparing their nests, while their mates, their duty to life fulfilled for this year, lounge at the entrance to their burrows. Alternately they sit upright or crouch in the sunlight, now and then emitting their piercing warning whistles if they imagine some danger. Near the homes of these creatures, the pastel bodies of the chipmunks are quick shapes as they scurry across the forest floor seeking needed food. And the females of this species are also preparing to give life to the wilderness.

The foxes, too, have mated. With the vixens busy in their dens, the dogs hunt. All the while the creatures they seek, the small things of the forest, are hiding and birthing their young, for this is spring, the time of life, of many new miracles of Creation; and nowhere is it more active than in the area of my lake, that place where the water lilies grow.

What of the lake itself? What is happening around its banks and under its murky waters? These are difficult questions that I have set for myself.

In that small lake of mine, a million-million flecks of life are stirring as energetically as are the creatures that live in the free space above the water. And countless plants, and fish, and insects; and to tell fully of all of these would require a dozen books and an infinity of time. Yet I must try, if only in brief, to write of all these things, or the story of this lake would remain incomplete.

Of all the living things that abound in the water the lilies are the most striking, and the first of the flowers in spring, summer and autumn to be seen by a visitor. And they are beautiful. In some

places they grow in small clusters, in others they cover the water with a vast, green-shiny matting of great leaves from amongst which the cups of the perfect blooms emerge during summer. There are two varieties of these plants on my lake, the yellow and the white, each distinct not only because of its colour, but also because of its shape. The yellow lily reflects the colour of pure butter in each of its three rounded petals and in its round, stubby heart. The white lily has more leaves and a smaller heart, which, like the entire bloom of its relative, is also golden yellow.

The plants root deep in the mud and, because it is necessary for the leaves and blooms to breathe free air, sinuous stems, long and flexible, emerge from the root tubers and drift upwards to the surface before unfurling the dark green leaves that always float on top of the water, even should its level climb or drop. This is because of the flexible stem, designed carefully for just this purpose, which, during low-water time in midsummer, trails loosely like some hank of submerged rope, only to straighten when fresh rains raise the level of the lake. Thus we find more evidence of Creation's careful planning. If the stem of these lilies were rigid, such as are the stems of land plants, low water would find the leaves and flowers suspended above the fluid with which they must always be in contact if they are to survive.

Beautiful they are, but they have been designed for more than the aesthetic admiration of man. From as far south as the gulf of Mexico to as far north as the Gulf of St Lawrence, these lilies furnish life not only to birds and mammals, but also to the ponds in which they grow, for during the autumn their slippery stems and their giant leaves die and disintegrate in the water. Slowly, these lilies, helped by other aquatic plants, build soil on the bottom of the lake from the broken-down remains of their stems, leaves and flowers, and more slowly yet, they build up the soil until it protrudes above the water, and a new cycle of life begins in the wilderness.

On their big leaves insects often rest and small birds land to sip lake water; frogs sun themselves on them in fix-eyed idleness that deceives insects to alight within reach of the sticky amphibian

Water lily leaves provide a resting spot for insects, a living sundeck for frogs.

tongues. Their seeds supply food for the ducks and geese and other water birds; their leaves and stems are fodder for the giant moose and for the beaver and the muskrat; their roots, tuberous and large, are food likewise for beaver and rat and moose. Even man may eat these roots as they make a good substitute for potatoes and were, many years ago, one of the main staples of the Aboriginal peoples. In the shade of their leaves, small fish find shelter and bigger fish lurk and hunt, while on the underside of the leaves, amongst the slime that adheres to them, tiny water life clings and finds sustenance amongst the invisible food organisms that also grow there.

The yellow lily, or brandy bottle, as it is also called, smells of alcohol and, during summer, it scatters its seeds in an unusual way. When I first witnessed this, even I wondered what was taking place around me, and it was more by coincidence than design that I noticed what this strange plant was doing. I had been restless. The moon was full and I left Joan asleep while I went for a walk. Inevitably I walked to the lake, for it was one of those nights when the moon on water draws a restless man as irresistibly as a magnet draws steel filings.

As I walked the summer night crackled. Mice moved, hares galloped and the stealthy pads of raccoons were audible in the

underbrush. A wolf howled, throwing his melancholia at the moon. The scene was invigorating, the stars had gentle green eyes that looked benignly upon the forest. Halfway to the lake, a great grey owl spoke to me in that deep bass which characterizes the bird. The forest was alive and I was no less so. Even the droning mosquitoes had no power to lessen the adventure of my walk.

I reached the lake and I held my breath. A person must experience the infinite solitude of the wilderness to appreciate my feelings when my eyes beheld the glories of that small, insignificant pond alight with the yellow of moonglow. No breath of wind ruffled the water; the stars shimmered in its depth; the fat, round moon looked up from its surface. A whip-poor-will called and frogs and toads massed their chorused voices, while the smell of pine was fragrant perfume in the air and the acid smell of mud and decaying vegetation at the lake's edge were spices which blended the whole. And then I heard the first gentle 'pop.'

This was a foreign sound. I remained still while I listened for another like it; and soon it came, and was quickly followed by another, and yet another, until it seemed that the entire surface of the lake was frothing from these small explosions. Subconsciously, I began to search in my mind for the creature that could be responsible for this noise, but no mammal or bird that I knew of had ever been credited with these gentle pops.

Then the noise was repeated almost at my feet and, as I gazed at the water, I actually saw a yellow brandy bottle as it burst its pod and scattered its seeds upon the surface of the lake, to the accompaniment of that mysterious little pop. I was intrigued, wondering why these gourd-shaped pods were exploding, not yet realizing that it is the force with which the pregnant capsule bursts itself that scatters the seeds. The whole thing is logical enough when one stops to consider it, but this was a new experience for me. And it took me upwards of an hour to piece together the whys and wherefores of the brandy bottle's explosive powers. Since that time I have heard these miniature bursts on many a night, but, strangely, I have never after sun-up. Early morning, yes, but never after sun-up. Can it be that the blooms require the heat of the sun in order to begin a process of fermentation that slowly expands them and, when night cools them, causes them to fracture? I know not, but one day I hope to solve this puzzle.

Later, during a night of blackness in early spring, I witnessed a small drama as it unfolded upon the submerged part of one of the lily leaves. The snow had left early and with visible speed, and water coursed freely through the entire forest, soaking slowly into frost-hard earth and accelerating the season by some three weeks. The lake was shrouded in fine mist, the gurgle of running water furnished the only music to this soggy, quiet night.

By the lakeshore I played aimlessly the beam of my flashlight, interested in the seeming-solidity of light thrust abruptly into a fog-filled atmosphere. Idly, I turned the light towards the water at my feet and some of it spilled on to the lily leaf, still young and only partly unfurled, the end where it developed from the stem forming a small, submerged cup. In this cup, the wriggling pink body of a small earthworm was flailing in agony as the jaws of a hungry backswimmer bit ravenously into it. Here was a strange battle. One which I had never before witnessed. The backswimmer, a predatory water insect, was perhaps half an inch long; the earthworm probably measured two inches. But the unfortunate worm had no equipment with which to defend itself against the ravishing of the insect; all it could do was wriggle in agony, jerking its pink string of a body in the hope of freeing itself from the predatory beak of the backswimmer. And then I saw that the insect was actually eating its victim alive!

When I first noticed the drama, the insect held the worm with its jaws and seemed to be using its victim's frenzy as an aid in tearing the flesh. Then, it reached forward with its forelegs and held the worm's body while it let go with its jaws. Although I could not actually see its chewing action, it plainly swallowed its mouthful and then again sank its beak into the worm, immediately letting go with its forelegs. Several minutes later, evidently replete, it released the unfortunate worm and left the scene, turning onto its

back to swim away, using its hind legs like miniature, but effective oars. In an instant it was gone. Its victim, no doubt washed into the water by the spring flood, slowly wriggled off the leaf in an attempt to reach land, its lacerated end showing the beak marks of the beetle.

This was just one small incident in the life of my lake, but it revealed to me yet another creature of these waters which, until then, I had seen often enough, but which I had invariably taken for granted, not giving it more than a casual thought. But, small as were both participants in the drama, the power of that primitive battle for survival was such that I was driven to learn more about backswimmers.

There are six varieties of these creatures living in North America; all belong to the family *Notonectidae*. As a rule they are about half an inch in length, of drab grey colour on the back, while their undersides, most commonly seen, are patterned with light green. They have three legs on each side of their bodies and these are graded in length and have different uses. The smallest of these are the front legs, which the insects use for grasping their prey; the longer, middle pair are used for grasping objects in the water or on land, while the back ones, the longest of all, are their oars and are flattened and furnished with stiff hair to increase their swimming powers. Their eyes are huge, situated on either side of the head, fairly well forward, and their 'face' is fashioned into a wicked-looking green beak. The compound eyes guide them in search of victims through the murky depths of lake, or stream or puddle; the horny beak with its tapered jaws provides the armament for an insect that can inflict painful bites upon most creatures; even on man.

Under the water, the backswimmers carry their own supply of air trapped by hairs which grow in two grooves on the lower end of their abdomen. Out of the water, they are driven by capable wings during night flights, their take-off power being furnished by the strong back legs, which lift them free of the water and allow them to spread their wings. Voracious in appetite, backswimmers prey on small fish, tadpoles, worms and other aquatic

insects. They breed by copulation and the females glue their eggs on plants or bury them in plant tissue. Naturally, they are themselves preyed upon by larger fish and by birds.

The duel I witnessed that night between the backswimmer and the worm was equal in stark savagery to any of the most spectacular battles between large mammals. And yet, as is so often the case, I almost missed it because my instincts prompted me to look for the more obvious events around me. This is the habit of people (one which I am fortunately breaking), who are so busy seeking grandiose experience that they often miss the real dramas of life.

In recent years, I have often been amazed at the abysmal ignorance of my fellows in things natural. Biologically-speaking, many otherwise-well-educated men and women show sheer illiteracy in the affairs of our earth and I have noticed that the more preoccupied and frustrated that these people become, the less attention they focus on the natural miracles of life, undoubtedly believing that man, having achieved the pinnacle of superiority over all other creatures, need no longer concern himself with the 'lower orders.' And often it is these same people, who, when exposed to the wilderness and properly introduced to it, express the most amazement at the wonders of creation.

Chasing that chimera which we call happiness has become humanity's greatest concern and the biggest source of un happiness. Perhaps this is because we have lost sight of ourselves; because we think of ourselves as *people* and set ourselves apart from animals which, most of us feel, are beneath us. Indeed, when a person wishes to describe the grossest members of his kind he all-too-frequently calls them animals, unwittingly insulting himself (for, like it or not, man is an animal in the strict sense of the word), and showing crass ignorance in the affairs of Creation.

Each man, consciously or unconsciously, feels himself to be a bit of a god. Seldom does he stop to consider that he is cousin to the gorilla, and the chimpanzee, the baboon and the lemur, to name but a few of our relatives. He often is not aware that he is but one of more than one million other species, a small, puny

being compared to the enormous sperm whale; a towering, invincible giant in comparison to the tiny protozoa. Unlike his wild relatives, he is so taken up in self-admiration that he often is unable to appreciate the immensely-wonderful, vastly-fascinating, beautiful world of Creation to which he is inexorably bound; to which he will one day return; which will in the end take his seemingly useless carcass and convert it into new energy; from which will spring plants and trees and insects and bacteria and birds and mammals, and even his own kind. For the death which he believes is the end of all things, is, in reality, only the beginning; the start of one more inevitable cycle; one more intricate phase of that very same Creation which sparked life on this planet earth so many millions of years ago...but let us return to my lake!

Playing their savage games of tag around the lilies, the water shrews chitter and dive and surface again, then scurry across the big leaves, forever hungry, forever seeking a frog, or a fish or an insect upon which to pounce, while now and then the killer-jaws of a northern pike snap shut upon the nimble little murderers. And it was thus one morning in late April, and I witnessed the killing. The sun was still a red glow of promise when I reached the lake and found a seat upon a round granite boulder, settling myself for an hour's peace by the water.

For a time I watched a blackbird cock through my field glasses as he balanced delicately upon the topmost branches of a poplar and sang his mating chant. Half-spreading his black wings, the twin patches of scarlet and yellow upon his shoulders brilliant winglets of colour flashing resplendently, he wooed his demure brown hen. And then the shrill scream of a shrew drew my attention to the water. I searched the nearby shore with the glasses and presently spotted the shiny-smallness of the killer. He was balanced on a lily leaf as the glasses picked him up, but in a flash he was gone into the water with one of the lightning-quick, overboard dives in which these little creatures specialize. As quickly he was up again, on another leaf, then he left his living raft and actually walked across the top of the water, the minute air bubbles clinging

to his feet allowing him this privilege. I actually saw the green-yellow jaws of the pike break water and engulf the shrew. One moment there it was, a tiny being of seeming magic as it ran carefree upon the lake's surface, then it was no more, the only sign of its presence the fast-spreading turbulence left by the predator head and jaws of the killer-fish.

When nature dispenses such instant death the delicate sensitivities of man often become offended. My own are no exception. But instants after the pike had so swiftly killed the shrew, my eyes beheld new life and I was struck by the almost ironical method with which Creation rules her world. Still retaining the mental image of that splash of death, I set down the glasses and stared idly at a cluster of bur reeds that grew in the water a few feet from where I was.

Clinging to one of the plant's ribbon-like leaves was an insect nymph. And by its actions I knew that it was about to transform itself, to emerge from its old skin and display its new self to the wilderness. I watched, and infinitely slowly the dragonfly nymph rippled and the scaly skin along its back began to split and now the new insect began to show, the dark hue of its body arching out of the brittle old skin like some miniature bridge. The head emerged and one leg; then a second leg. Now the fly began working itself out of the nymphal skin. At last the whole insect appeared. It paused on its disused 'skeleton' and seemed to survey the newness that surrounded it. Then, crawling over the skin and feeling hesitatingly for the surface of the leaf, it settled there, somehow knowing that it must wait for the sun to dry the gossamer of its finely-veined wings before it should attempt to fly. My eyes remained glued to it. Soon the transparent wings began to vibrate, slowly at first, then faster and faster, until their movement was but a vague blur. And then, lifting like a tiny helicopter, the dragonfly essayed its first flight and the sunlight awoke its body. Irridescent green and copper flashed delicately, and fine-spun silver sparkled from wings etched with a tracery of ebony lines. Away it went, the slight rustle of its dry wings music; a new life being greeted by a new day in spring.

The shrew and the dragonfly: life and death; the basic ingredients of this squat sphere we call earth. The former we understand a little, the latter we know not and we fear greatly. Inevitably, each animate thing upon this planet will be touched by both: the beginning, and the end. But it is what lies in between that counts, or should count! And it is that which interests me these days and the knowledge that I have begun my beginning and that I am heading towards my end has sharpened my greed for knowing, and has all but entirely removed the old superstitious dread with which I once regarded death. Today, it is enough that I am here, alive and able to observe the bustle of creation that constantly changes with wilderness, felling a tree here, planting a seed there. A hunter strikes and kills; a bird lays an egg. Drought seres a crust of earth; rain comes to recreate it. Can there be a more satisfying way of living for a man interested in life?

Nowadays, it seems, I am so full of things about which I want to tell that I sometimes don't know which I should write first. Now, for instance: which comes first, the plant or the insect? The plant, I think, for it was the bur reed that hosted the dragonfly, and the bur reed is a permanent part of the lake, while the insect, a feather-light bit of natural colour, may leave this place and die on some other body of water.

Bur reeds haunt the shallows of lakes or marshes, thrusting their coarse, ribbon leaves two and three feet above the water and playing host to many insects and larder to birds and animals. The plant grows male and female flowers; the latter quite large, spiky growths occupying solitary space on the roundish, fat stems; the former, small, speckly-round objects that cluster six and more to a stem, for there are more males than females living on this plant. Between June and August, the female flowers are ready to accept the male pollen which is blown upon them by the wind. And if these water plants cannot compete for beauty with their neighbours, the lilies, still they are pleasant and artistically designed, rimming the lake with their sober green and their golliwog's-head female blooms that are topped by the speckled male clusters. And

they are useful too, offering themselves to the creatures of the lake; to the birds, who go them; to the muskrats and the beaver, who munch off their stems; to the deer and the moose, who browse them for nourishment and moisture; to the dragonfly nymph, who crawled up on thick stem from the depth of the lake and used the plant for its transformation.

The insect belonged to the *Aeshnid* family of dragonflies, more poetically known as 'the devil's darning needle,' because, folklore has it, the dragonflies of this species sewed up the ears of small boys who had been naughty! Still they are dragonflies, and thus follow the traditional lines of these insects; the huge eyes, the double pair of transparent wings, the short bristly antennae, the squat chest leading to the long slender body. Beauty graces the adult flies, and a great ravenous hunger for mosquitoes and other small insects characterizes the species. Between the pinnacles of aestheticism and predatory urge, there is a valley of strange fascination. And it begins with the creature's life under the murky waters.

Wrote Virgil: "The descent of Avernus is easy; the gate of Pluto stands open night and day; but to retrace one's steps and return to the upper air—that is toil; that the difficulty." Publius Vergilius Maro, the Roman poet born in 70 BC, was not thinking of the dragonfly when he captured that bit of philosophy. He was describing man's seeming determination to explore the pit of Hell, embodied, so the ancients believed, within the depth of Lake Avernus. But Virgil (or Vergil, as he is variously named) unwittingly captured the spirit of the dragonfly's life cycle.

It is, indeed, easy for the creature to make the descent of Avernus, and thereafter it must toil mightily to retrace its steps to the upper air, where its journey really begins. There, during spring and summer adult 'darners' mate, the male and female flying locked in a complex manoeuvre, the performance of which is similar to the techniques so recently adopted by man for refuelling an aircraft in mid-air.

When a female of the species exhibits her readiness for the mating, she is grasped by the back of her head by the male, who uses special 'grappling' hooks for the purpose. The two insects continue flying while a strange form of copulation occurs, for the male's reproductive organs are carried in separate parts of his body, the copulation organ being placed below the second joint of his body while his sperm duct openings are located on the lower side of the ninth body segment. In mid-air, grasping the female by the head, the male dragonfly must transfer a capsule of sperm from his ninth body segment to his second body segment. When he has done this, the female he is towing curves her abdomen into a hook and brings its tip into contact with the male's second body section, accepting the capsule into her body. There, the male's sperm is released from the capsule and is able to fertilize the waiting eggs. The pair then go their separate ways.

The male streaks jauntily across the lake, seeking prey; the female goes to lay her eggs, which she may deposit on the surface of the water, on the leaves and stalks of water plants, or actually within the tissues of certain plants, depending on the species of dragonfly. When the eggs hatch, the baby nymphs descend into their own particular Avernus, there to swim and hunt and change their size by the process of outgrowing the old skin from ten to fifteen times during a year or more of aquatic living.

If the adult flies are beautiful, their nymphs or naiads, are the diametric opposite! They look vaguely like some Egyptian mummy that has escaped its sarcophagus to go crawling along the lake bottom, dressed in honey-coloured bandages upon strange, lanky legs. Out of its back protrude stubby wing capsules, functionless deformities that enhance the grotesque aspect of the runaway. If beauty lurks anywhere upon the body of this strange beast, it hides in the large dark, oval eyes. But these, the creature's best features, can do little to offset a gargoyle of a face furnished with a pointed beak, the lower 'lip' of which is three times longer than the entire head and is hinged in such a manner that the insect can shoot it out to swiftly grasp a victim and draw it into its mouth. So long is this lip that, when it is not in use, it must be wrapped over the mouth and over a part of the face, giving the nymph a masked appearance if it is seen at rest. And as though these oddities were not enough, the creature has managed to acquire yet another singular characteristic! It breathes through gills, rather like a fish, but these gills are not carried in the conventional place, being instead located in a large chamber that grows into the body out of the creature's rectum.

These strange little monsters (big, actually, for an insect, measuring up to two inches in length) spend most of their waking time prowling the lake bottom in search of victims, propelling themselves along by ejecting jets of water through the strangely-situated gill chamber. And anything small enough to be subdued serves as food for the dragonfly nymph.

Dragonflies have been around for a long time. In fact, the ancestors of today's insects were veritable giants, with a wingspan of up to two feet, that flew in the skies of 275 million years ago! And since that time, but for a drastic reduction in size, they have changed not at all, though we do not know what their eating habits were then. Today, the adult flies seem to prefer mosquitoes and blackflies and for this reason they have been christened 'mosquito hawks.' These flies hunt on the wing. Their legs are weak and little suited for perching, but they are equipped with fine long hairs; zipping along through the air, the dragonfly swoops on its victim, making a scoop out of its hairy legs, catching its prey in it, then holding the catch there while it eats, still flying.

Of course, as do all creatures, dragonflies have enemies. In the water their nymphs are eaten by fish and turtles; in the air they are devoured by birds, especially by the pigeon hawk. But provided that man does not do something to destroy them, dragonflies are not in danger of extermination. They have been around long enough to learn the tricks of survival as a species and, from spring until the harsher frosts of autumn herald the coming of winter, the wilderness day is a-buzz with the sound of their wings while their flashing, iridescent bodies add quick touches of lush colour to lake and marsh and forest.

Because blood-sucking insects, such as the mosquito and the buffalo gnat, are drawn into the pursuit of their prey by the

warmth of the bodies of their intended victims, wild animals and people are usually surrounded by these pests during the 'fly months.' And because dragonflies feed on these blood suckers, the colourful mosquito hawks are not very far away at these times. They are always welcome sight to me then, for if there are always enough pests to make life a bit miserable when I am out in the summer bush, still it is a comfortable thing to know that four or five dragonflies are busy over my head, devouring the creatures that are seeking my blood. Science today has furnished us with some very effective fly repellents, a supply of which I always take with me into the wilderness. This blessed spray, succinctly called 'Off' by its makers, does a wonderful job in keeping at bay the mosquitoes and the deer flies and the horse flies; and even the pesky, tenacious buffalo gnats, or blackflies, as they are also called. But these tiny, hump-backed feeders on blood have some nasty habits that 'Off' cannot defeat.

They stray away from exposed skin areas sprayed by the repellent, but when one least expects them, they crawl cunningly between clothing and body and with great stealth insert their sucking tubes. The result, later, is an angry-red volcano of skin with a purplish bulls-eye, in the centre of which is a red puncture mark. And an itch. A great, sadistic, finger-nail-tempting itch that clamours to be scratched and turns into a dull throb when it has had its way. Unpleasant? Definitely. But one learns to live with these things when one seeks the wilderness, and even the pesky black flies have a part to play in the forest.

In size these deformed little monsters measure one eighth of an inch or less; they have big round eyes and short, but very effective, sucking-piercing mouths. Of course, the female of the species is deadlier than the male; in fact, as is the case with the mosquito, it is only the female that sucks blood, but their voracity is such that no warm-blooded animal is safe from them. And the species is prolific!

Depending on the kind of gnat, the eggs range in colour from yellow to black; they are minute little bits of life which are deposited by the females in large masses on wet rocks, on plants that grow in or near fast-moving water, on damp, rotting logs or even submerged in the water. When the tiny larvae hatch from the eggs, they come equipped to face a hostile world. They are fitted with a suction disc and with stiff little hooked hairs on each end of their bodies. With these they can defeat water current, swimming about over rocks and vegetation and occasionally attaching their suction cups to some anchored object and standing on their tails in the water. In addition to this, they carry their own lifeline, for they have the ability to spin a thread which they can attach to rock or plant by means of which they can swim happily in swift waters. At this stage both male and female are omnivorous, devouring minute microscopic plants and animal matter which they sweep into their chewing mouths by means of two specialized little scoops.

Six times the larvae shed their skins before they finally pupate inside a silken cocoon, spun and affixed to a sunken rock or plant, the top end of which is left open. One would think that Creation had helped these little brutes sufficiently by this time; but, no. There is one more aid that has been supplied them. When the adult gnat finally emerges from the cocoon it does so under water and, though during its infancy it was equipped with breathing gills, as an adult it breathes normally and would drown if it did not have a means of getting air on the way up. So, before the larva begins to pupate, it somehow works an air bubble into its cocoon. When the adult is born, it leaves its underwater nest by means of its own escape air chamber, inside of which it rides out its upward journey. On the surface, it takes to its wings immediately and flies away, and if it be a female it at once seeks a feed of fresh, warm blood.

Fortunately, the gnat season is short, consisting mainly of six or seven weeks in late spring and early summer and, in the far north, recurring again for a few weeks during the autumn. And life is not always easy for these creatures. All insect-eating birds feast on them; many other insects besides the dragon and damsel flies eat of them; and infinitesimal micro-organisms called mematodes

parasitize their bodies. Still they are a part of Creation, a part of my lake and, persistent and troublesome though they are, yet they are interesting little creatures who have the grace to disappear quickly; which is more than can be said for the mosquitoes, the females of which lie in wait from the first day of spring until frost drives them away in late summer.

Yet, Creation always seems to have an answer for everything and animals constantly exposed to the bites of these insects acquire some degree of immunity to their attacks—though, if the insects are numerous enough, they can kill an animal by the simple process of sucking it dry—and man is no exception to this. During the years that I have been exposed to mosquitoes, I have found that inflammation of the bites decreases with exposure. And of recent years I am even acquiring some resistance to the bite of the buffalo gnat.

Still I am glad when the sun rises hot and strong in summer and sends both these pests scurrying for shade, for, like all creatures that live on salty blood, their heat tolerance is low. They would dehydrate if they remained exposed to sunlight, knowledge of which man can use to good effect around the area of his dwellings by keeping the grass short and thus reducing their moist hiding places.

Still, these creatures are as much a part of my lake as are the lilies and the beaver and all the other forms of life that abound there. Unpleasant they are, at times, but they are necessary evils which Creation, in its wisdom, has placed on earth. As such they must be accepted.

EIGHT

NOW IT IS LATE MAY. The sun is warm, the grasses are lush and green and the lilies peep from the lake water, the white and yellow of their faces not yet fully open to the new season. It is evening, almost; but there is yet sun to glow over the area, to warm the bones. At the north end of the lake there is a large granite boulder, rounded and scarred from centuries of weather, splashed by the limey manure of birds, decorated by tiny black droppings of squirrels, wetted by the urine of wolves. This boulder is a wolf scent station, a place that must be called on by each passing pack, smelled, inspected, then wetted, so that others coming later will know who has passed this way.

On this evening of flaming sun and clear blue sky, a long dog wolf lurks in the shadow of the boulder. He has not sniffed or wetted, for he is here intent upon another purpose. He plans to kill this day and his victim is a big male beaver, an old beaver, made sluggish by age and the parasites that infest his seventy-pound body. The wolf has spent a week in the area and has killed mice and marmots while watching the beaver, learning of its habits, planning his attack. And this is the day for the killing; now the wolf knows the ritual of his victim, so he waits, hungry, patient, intent, a killing machine coiled and ready to spring.

In the water the old beaver is swimming slowly northwards. He has been away from his den but ten minutes and is now intent on his careful journey to his feeding grounds, the marsh of catkins on the east bank of the lake. To reach it he must leave the water for a few yards, lumber slowly over the rocky shore and pass the boulder before flopping again into water. The wolf knows this.

The sun is fading now; the shadows are longer, they help conceal the lurking wolf. He lies doglike, haunches curled under, forelegs out straight ahead, a living statue made of lithe muscle and heavy bones. The strength of him shows clearly in the deep chest, the graceful neck, the broad head with its high forehead and big intelligent eyes. He is young, this forest marauder, and healthy, one of creation's perfect executioners who now waits intent for the creature that has been condemned by time. He knows the moment of the killing will soon be here and every nerve in his being is trigger-taut as the hunting instincts of centuries dominate him, keep him there immobile, though his excitement is so great that he wants to whine his eagerness. He swallows his voice and waits, an integral part now of the scene.

You who read this may find it in you now to hate this killer wolf, to fear him, even though you sit in your comfortable chair in the security of your home, a civilized creature with pity in your heart for him who is about to die. Don't. Don't hate this courageous animal. Don't pity his victim. The beaver must die, that is inevitable. How much quicker and cleaner will be his death at the jaws of the wolf? And of the hunter? Think about him, you there in your safe seat! Put yourself in his place, bring your mind here and see him, feel the tension of this place, experience the urgency that grips this wolf!

Cast from your mind the sweet, childish untruths of 'Little Red Riding Hood' and 'The Three Little Pigs,' for, maligned though he has been by man, the wolf is not the symbol of evil. He does not constantly lust for food; he does not kill wantonly. Creation ordained that he should be thus and fashioned him well, and having done this, released him upon earth. And then came man and turned him into a pariah. Man, the most ruthless killer of them all, the most pitiless, the most vicious and intelligent, came. Perhaps he envied the grace and freedom and courage of this great beast and he tried, for century after century, to subdue him, to bend his will, for man was the king of beasts. But the wolf would not be subdued. He remained free and courageous and honest and we hated him for it. And because he resisted us, because, despite all our best efforts, he continued to survive in the fastness of his wilderness, we turned him into a villain.

It takes great courage, and intelligence and endurance, to be a wolf and live. Consider: the hand of almost every man is turned against him; he lives from kill to kill, enjoys, today a glut, tomorrow a rib-sculpting famine. He must be satisfied most of the time with tiny kills, mice and moles and perhaps an occasional hare, though he may weigh as much as 170 pounds, and must lope and gallop for hours at a time, even often fruitlessly, to lie down hungry and spent under some downed tree to wait for a new night and a new ordeal. It may well be that he will bed again hungry, come dawn. To retain the spark of life in a man-free wilderness is in itself a feat for such as he. To survive the guns of man, his vicious leg traps and his poison baits, and then to face with equanimity the uncertainties of forest living requires special courage, and skill and a constitution of iron. In winter, it is the great cold and the scarcity of game and the long wearisome journeys through a killer land, tail tucked despondently between straining flanks, belly shrunken against the pain of hunger, reduced to the fruitless chewing of frozen tree bark. Or, if luck is with him, it may be the discarded antler of deer or moose or even the droppings of his own kind, manure pellets that contain little sustenance, for such a creature must digest every atom of protein swallowed, and his body uses all but chips of bone and the indigestible fur of the creatures he has hunted. And then, when death has almost become a friend, a kill is made and life flows again. This is the life of the timber wolf; this is the wolf, a creature fiercely loyal to his own, capable of a depth of affection perhaps stronger than a person's, certainly more selfless and sacrificing.

He waits this evening, eager, hungry, indomitable. And now he can hear the old beaver which has surfaced two hundred yards away and is swimming tired towards the landing place. A slight quiver betrays the tensions gripping him. The beaver swims closer, hesitates, turns away to paddle an infinitely slow half circle in the water, searching the land with habitual care.

In the sky above a big ebony bird glides effortlessly over the lake. The turkey vultures have returned for another year and the male is quartering his territory seeking carrion. His ugly head, naked and scarlet and wrinkled, twists constantly from side to side as the piercingly-keen eyes search the forest floor. The vulture sees the beaver and he circles the lake while the water creature seeks signs of danger. Can the scavenger of the skies detect death already?

The wolf sees the vulture, but not by the movement of one hair does he betray his presence to the black bird. One slight flick of an ear, one involuntary lift of the head: either will be quickly spotted by the vulture, who will turn in his circle to investigate. This would be warning enough for the beaver, who has also seen the bird and knows that by watching him he can detect the presence of an enemy.

A tableau: The sun gone and leaving a faint ruby glow on the western sky; the lake sprawled darkly within its cleft of granite, its waters stilled and dull, the broad green lily pads shiny-wet, the delicate blooms furled for the night, oval buttons of yellow and white. The song of the frogs intermittent on the air; the buzzing drone of the mosquito pitches a constant huskiness. The beaver rippling through the water, in straight line now, making for the rock. The wolf immobile. The vulture sailing into the distance, a small black dot against the northern twilight. For a moment there is peace.

The beaver reaches the landing place, pauses a moment, half in and half out of the water, moisture dripping from his dark flanks, small ears cupped for sound, nostrils testing for scent. Within the body of the hunting wolf the tension goes. Now the beast is relaxed, easy, yet muscles and sinews are ready for instant action, for only ten feet separate him from his victim.

The beaver moves again, climbing the rock slope slowly. One step, two, a trail of wet following the paddle tail, little sticks and bits of last year's leaves sticking to the low-slung belly and flanks, matting in the long, silken fur. Two more steps as the webbed back feet follow the wet traces of the front paws; now a pause, more movement forward.

The wolf springs. He moves so quickly it would be impossible to see his action. One instant he is there, prone and still, the next his flashing fangs and gaping mouth are but inches above the beaver, reaching already for the back of the neck; and if the victim's reflexes have already signalled the doomed creature to turn towards the water, the message from the brain centre to the limbs has come too late. There is a low growl that mingles with a shrill squeal of fear and the beaver is clamped within the vice of long canines that arm the hunter. Now a quick shake of the wolfish head, an audible snap as the beaver's neck breaks. Nothing more, the killing is done; the beaver's lifeless body jerks three times in the dance of death, his bowels and bladder discharge their last excretions. The wolf turns from the water with his victim dangling inertly, a dead weight, but carried easily by the timber wolf.

In a tangle of alders the hunter drops his victim. But he does not tear into the carcass right away, hungry though he is. Seeming to recognize that he has executed perfectly, he pauses to refresh his nostrils with the musky smell of the victim and drool falls from his parted mouth as anticipation excites his palate. He touches the warm, wet body with his nose; he dances a little, light jumps of eagerness, then he bows to his victim, as though in salute, dropping his forelegs and chest to the ground, keeping his hindquarters upright for a moment. Now he settles to his meal. He bites, rips, gouges. The dark fur flies, the red blood flows, the wolf's lips and muzzle are stained by it.

STILL IT IS MAY beside the lake; the later now, for the month is almost over. In the marsh that used to be the feeding place of the old beaver there is a shape that looks like a small, rather squat Indian tepee. It is a muskrat house. Inside it crouches a female rat and she is about to begin the birthing of her first litter of this season.

The mounded house that she built here is near the edge of land, but yet surrounded by water, for safety's sake, and there is a slim channel, of which the rat knows, that leads into the main body of the lake. Two years ago this she-rat came here, an outcast

EIGHT

from her mother's lodge, seeking a good place upon which to build her refuge. She found it on a small mound of decaying timber and vegetation that had accumulated on the silty marsh floor and had almost thrust itself above the level of the water. On this mound she scooped mud and sticks and grasses, until she had raised it to a height of two feet and given it a base three feet in circumference. Satisfied, she went underwater and began carving into the mound, using teeth and front paws to make an underwater tunnel into the centre of it, then biting and pulling and scraping until she reached above the water level. Now she excavated a round chamber. This was her lodge, completed when she had carved out a second tunnel, on the opposite side to the first, for it is always necessary to have an emergency escape exit. It had been late autumn when her house was finished and within its shelter she had awaited the arrival of winter and, when it had come, she had fared well, sleeping comfortably, eating, keeping alive.

At last had come spring and she had mated. Her first litter was born in this place and was ejected to make room for the second birthing, and these young ones were also ejected to make room for her third litter of the year. And then had come another autumn, and another winter, and spring again; and the female rat mated again, and went through the same routing and another year passed. Now she was about to give birth to her seventh litter.

In the intervening seasons her small lodge had grown. Now it measured seven feet across at the bottom and stood nearly four feet high and her bedchamber was fourteen inches long and eleven inches wide. At opposite ends of this room were two old beds, wet bundles of shredded bulrush leaves mixed with grass and rootlets that she had ferried here for her sleeping comfort. One bed was fresh, the other moulding; both were wet, but this was of no concern to the water rat. After the birthing she would change the moulding vegetation, but the new materials would arrive here soaked from their journey under the water.

The muskrat is now gripped by the spasms of birth pains. They seize her body quickly, squeeze it as her pelvic muscles contract and release it again. She hunches her back in the darkness, trying to ease the hurt, then she waits for the next onslaught, while deep within her body, encased in the tube-like womb, seven tiny kits are waiting their time to emerge. Each is fully formed; each has begun to struggle to free itself from the sausage-like casing that surrounds it. For thirty days these mites have been attaining form in the female rat's womb.

Their journey to life began with the union of their parents, when the male rat, with whom the female had mated, his invisible sperm discharged into her body. If seen under a microscope, each would have resembled a little black claw from the base of which flowed a long, very thin tail. A host of these strange little germs did the male rat inject into the female: seven of them reached seven eggs that were waiting inside. Each penetrated one egg, completing its journey to its resting place by wildly flailing its thin tail, propelling itself thus, a thing impossible to see with the naked eye yet still a creature of life, already involved in competition with its fellows. For only a few could unite with the waiting eggs, and those that reached their target too late would die in the female's womb and slowly slide out to the world again, dead things embalmed in the body fluids of the female. Their only hope now of taking part in the affairs of earth is the chance that the waste fluids might fertilize some tiny patch of soil, from which would grow a plant and into the body of which the dead sperm would merge, after the soil and the things of the soil had reconstructed them into new energy.

As soon as the seven male germs thrust their ways through the walls of the eggs, Creation began engineering seven little muskrats. The first happening was the division of the contents of each egg into two equal cells; then these cells split again and became four; then they split again, and now there were eight. And each cell continued splitting until hundreds of cells were thus formed, and these banded together and became a rounded mass, hollow in the centre. Now only the outer skin remained of each of the original eggs; each held the ball of life made up of these split

cells. Each ball now began by pushing in a section of its wall until this inverted bump touched the opposite wall and the round ball became a U-shaped mass inside its oval skin. In the cavity, between the two prongs of the U were to form, in time, the stomachs and intestines of the baby rats. Now the embryo is attainting some semblance of animal shape; it 'eats' through the navel cord, grows daily and begins its first sluggish movements: little jerks that are visible on one of the mother's flanks as her developing babies alter position in her womb. Already these babies have functional hearts and all their many complex organs are taking shape. And in the miraculously short span of only thirty days, the baby rats are fully formed, each weighing about three-quarters of an ounce and measuring a scant four inches in length, counting their little tails. And this is the day that they are to emerge into their world of water and darkness, and fear, and death and mating-lust.

The rat is seized by a rigid spasm. She can feel the first of her babies sliding along the womb towards her opening as the muscles squeeze. She is allowed a short rest. Now another seizure and she helps this time, forcing, pushing with all her might and the baby, still encased in its birth cowl, slides free and falls on to the cold, damp floor of the nest chamber. While she waits for the next seizure, the mother rat twists her face towards her new child and licks it, breaking the birth cowl and giving air to her offspring. And one by one, announced by seizure after seizure, the baby rats are born, are licked, are cleaned. The mother frees each of its navel cord, eating it; then she draws them to her and they nurse while she rests and Creation cleans her womb of the membranes of birth, which slowly emerge from her opening. When the babies have fed, she cleans herself and removes the afterbirth by eating it also. New life has come to the rat's house. And death is already waiting outside.

Two of the baby muskrats died three days after they were born. The litter was suckling when the she-muskrat rose to her feet and left the lodge. Five of the babies let slip the nipples from their mouths; two held fast, hungry and stubborn, and they trailed the

mother, attached firmly to her as she plunged down one exit tunnel and began swimming under water. Now the kits let go. The female continued swimming. Behind her, tumbling and struggling, the kits drifted up to the surface.

Above the lake a marshhawk was gliding. He saw the kits, banked a steep turn and seized one of them. The other was near a partly-submerged log and was able to crawl on to it, there to squeak fear, calling its mother who was still submerged and either had not noticed the fate of her young or had decided that seven babies were too many, and was content to let these two die. For five hours the baby rat huddled shivering on the log, squeaking, squeaking; an incessant little shrill cry that slowly faded as the baby became exhausted; and at last was stilled. Now it was dusk; the small kit was still alive, but remained immobile, a little ball of shock.

From the bowels of the lake, the horny bulk of a large snapping turtle paddled casually towards the surface. When it broke water it remained still for a moment, only the tip of its predatory beak breaking the surface as its nostrils snuffled air. Then the head broke through and the puncture-marks of nose scented the baby rat that crouched forlorn but six feet away. The turtle paddled to the log, the small muskrat was knifed by the cutting beak. It died and was eaten.

What of the turtle? What of this strange reptile that has survived for 200 million years and has changed but little during 150 million years? Undoubtedly, its ancestors shared the world of the hulking dinosaurs; were, in fact, already on earth when the first of these was spawned, and its ancestors were still on earth when the last of the ungainly giants perished. And they are still here, these strange creatures who lead a double life.

The creatures are odd, ugly, ungainly of gait upon land, but they are of tenacious disposition, savage in their own way and built like no other creature. Sometime during the dawn of creation turtles began to change their bodies from those of the reptiles that sired them. They needed armour, so they reinforced their reptilian scales, made them thicker, and then they grew their ribs outside of their bodies and fused these to their strong, heavy scales. Thus, above their bodies, the top shell, or carapace, serves as shelter and protection, while the lower shell, the plastron, provides belly armour second to none.

Having done all this, after exchanging the speed and freedom of the reptile for the cumbersome safety of their armour plate, turtles developed their double life, taking to the water for ease of transportation, leaving it to lay their eggs on land so that the energy of sunlight would provide the needed warmth for incubation. Then, having done all these things with the help of Creation, they received one more boon. They were granted long life. Today some species are thought to live for as long as 150 years, while even comparatively small breeds have been known to survive in captivity for forty years and more, an exceptionally long span for a creature of the wilderness.

There are two kinds of these creatures inhabiting my lake. The gross, horny snapping turtle, the killer of the lake, and the pretty, more streamlined painted turtle. Both obey similar impulses during the spring season; they leave their water and make long journeys through the forest in search of suitable soil in which to dig a hollow and in which to lay from six to twelve eggs. This done, the soil is scraped back over the eggs and the turtles return to the water, content to allow nature the privilege of hatching their brood; their duty to life completed with the mating and the egg laying, their responsibility towards their offspring ended. They are uncaring of the toll that other creatures of nature take of their young, raccoons, for instance, and skunks, who love to dig up the eggs and devour them.

Inevitably, though, at least some of the turtles are born and manage to wobble their unsteady way to water through what to them must be obstacles of monumental proportions. But water they inevitably reach and there they are comparatively safe, for they have few enemies in that medium. At this time, they measure barely two inches in length and have probably hatched from eggs that would but poorly cover one inch of space. Now, with their horny bills they tear vegetable matter and worms and insects, and sometimes small fish, growing steadily, if slowly, over the years, gaining weight in body and shell, until they reach maturity some five or six years later. Then they make their spring trek to the egg-laying grounds, and back to the lake they go, creatures that now measure some eighteen inches across and weigh up to thirty-five or forty pounds, if they be snapping turtles; or attaining six inches in length and weighing a couple of pounds if they be of the painted variety.

I confess my dislike for the snapper! It seems such a treacherous beast, skulking in the shallows, waiting for duckling or adult duck, then moving upwards with surprising agility to grasp its victim by a leg and hold on until it has drowned the unfortunate creature. Its beak is a two-sided guillotine capable of inflicting severe punishment. Its head is an ugly thing punctuated by the twin nostrils and the horn-rimmed bulbous eyes. But even this creature of revulsion has its place in the scheme of the wilderness, and nowadays I try and abide by Creation's rules, so I let them live in my lake.

The common snapping turtle has ancestral roots dating back to the time of the dinosaurs.

It is two nights since the muskrat kits died. The lake is bathed by a full moon and there is no wind to pluck sound from the trees. The time is midnight; there is warmth in the air. High above the lake there is a sky that has been raked clean of cloud and is studded with a panoply of green winking stars. Silhouetted against the sky a great horned owl flaps over the lake in ghostly silence. On the lake and within its waters and along its shores, in the marshes that neighbour upon it, a veritable army of frogs and toads choruses a throbbing medley; the "basso" of the bullfrogs, the treble of the tree frogs; the tenor voices of the leopards and pickerels, the husky sopranos of the toads. Mingled with all these voices is the drone of the mosquitoes, while the occasional call of a brown-voiced owl supplies percussion to the concerto of the night.

The lake is a shimmering, peaceful place. Its placid water is now and then disturbed by the belly-flop of a frog leaping from a lily pad; here and there slow circles tell of a fish rising to breathe or to nibble some bit of forest waste that drifts across the surface. A raccoon is fishing from the eastern end of the beaver dam, dabbing swiftly at the water, each time his quick, agile fingers coming out dripping and grasping a small, wriggling minnow which he squeezes to death before laying it carefully on the mud of the dam. He has been fishing for almost ten minutes and has eight minnows lined up on land. He catches one more and this time sloshes it repeatedly in the water, enjoying the feel of it and of the moisture for a full minute before popping the morsel into his mouth. Now he feeds on the others, once interrupting his meal to 'wash' one minnow, but eating the rest without dunking them.

Out of the night two more raccoons come to join him, and at first he shows nervousness and is ready to back away; then he recognizes the smell of his two brothers and he waits for them. And the three fish side by side, like truant schoolboys enjoying a stolen outing. Afterwards they play, tumbling and rolling precariously on the narrow dam and one of them splashes into the lake to come bounding out, shaking water from his heavy coat. They wrestle some more, these three whelps from last spring's litter, too young to breed yet, not old enough to go their separate ways, still full of the zest of youth.

At last they tire of their game. One, the larger of the three, turns towards the western bank and gallops away, followed closely by the others, their run a seemingly-clumsy lope which is yet fast and agile. On the far bank they stop as through by pre-arrangement. The big fellow rears on his haunches momentarily, then launches himself upon one of his brothers; at once the third coon mixes in the fray and bites the right hind foot of his bigger brother. There is a growl, for the bite of those needle teeth hurts. The biter is cuffed and now it is his turn to growl and he goes for the big one's tail. Just as though it seems that there must be a fight, the three break and the leader again turns, this time ambling slowly towards a stand of tall poplars. He is again followed by the other two. In the shadows of the tall trees the raccoons almost disappear, for their striped fur was designed for this kind of country, ideal camouflage for these masked, playful rogues.

The smallest of the three starts climbing a poplar, gripping it bear-like, hands and arms reaching upwards, pulling; feet and legs digging into the tree's bark, pushing. He is two feet up when the big fellow stands upright and grips him by the ringed tail, pulling him down amid the scarping noise of claws resisting the pull against the tree. Again, there is a wrestling match and this one ends more swiftly than the others, for the three coons have heard a stranger approaching.

Now they stand immobile, the big one flanked by, and a little ahead of, the other two; three keen, inquisitive faces looking towards the slight noise made by some approaching creature. They smell the newcomer before they see it. A skunk comes, a male, rambling his nightly patrol through his piece of forest, slow, unafraid, partly full of insects and frogs, still seeking more food this night.

In a flash the three raccoons advance towards the skunk. They move in an inverted arrowhead, the big one in the centre; mischief is stamped over each rakish face. The skunk hears them coming and stops. It stamps its warning to the advancing raccoons, patting the ground with stiffened front legs while it alternately clicks its teeth and emits little growls of displeasure. Will the raccoons take fright and turn away from him? Not they! The bush gods made this their night for mischief and they love nothing better than skunk-baiting. Here is their chance.

Quickly they form a triangle around the skunk, who has now raised his bushy plume of a tail and is already set to discharge his musky spray. But at which of his tormentors should he aim? The skunk is an oldster, short of temper and more than ready to use his powerful liquid gas, but each time he bends his body into the U-position and begins to take aim at one raccoon, one of the other darts in quickly and slaps his head or flank. The skunk turns on the latest tormentor, bends into the U again and is quickly slapped by another raccoon, until at last in sheer exasperation and high rage, the skunk shoots through his twin musk glands, spraying his scent anywhere, pausing a fraction of time, turning and spraying again, while still the pestering trio pat and poke him from all sides. At last the skunk has soaked the three and even they must stop to catch their breath, for the musk is now so strong that it almost suffocates them. During the pause, the skunk trots away.

Now the three pranksters begin rolling on the forest floor, trying to remove the skunk's fetor and only succeeding in getting rid of the excess moisture. They reek of skunk spray, for they are thoroughly impregnated by the nauseous substance. Yet it does not appear to worry them unduly after they have regained their breath. They retrace their steps to the lake and enter the water and swim in it, again playful, biting at each other, pulling each other's tails, climbing on each other's backs. Then they leave the water and turn again towards the forest.

Ambling rumbustiously through the woods, the three hunt insects and worms, and if one finds a beetle or moth while the other two are empty-handed, he is crowded by his brothers while they try to steal his find. And he growls, seriously now, and occasionally a fight breaks out amongst them, a swift, biting and slashing fight that lasts but moments, but which is fierce and painful and draws blood from small cuts and claw-pricks. It ends as suddenly as it begins. The flight of a moth captures the attention of the combatants and the three turn in pursuit, dabbing with quick, dexterous paws, until the night flier is either captured or succeeds in making its escape.

While the smaller of the three raccoons is busy with a particular smell which he is enjoying, the others climb a nearby pine, going up in stealth, seeming to climb the vertical trunk on tiptoes, making not a sound. On the ground, the remaining brother abandons his sniffing and misses them and at once he feels panic, for these creatures are sociable when young and rely each upon the other. The lost one moves about nervously, undecided, his normal instincts deserting him so that he does not think to use his keen nose to trace the pathway of his brothers. Now he stops still and barks the raccoon panic cry: two short and staccato coughs issuing from deep down in the throat.

The two in the pine hear and peer down, still silent, appraising the situation. They see their brother and he is evidently unharmed and unmolested. They stare silently, not comprehending that it is their absence that has triggered the alarm cry, while the lonely one calls again and shuffles about aimlessly. Still his brothers look down on him and make no move to reassure him.

Yet, in the face of real danger, the alarm cry will quickly bring them to the rescue, unless the threatened one can make his escape, for they still remember the swift and savage reflexes of their mother when one of them made that small call. If later they will watch from safety while one of their own falls victim to predator or man, now they are still ready to defend each other. Fortunately, young raccoons are rarely forced to race to the rescue of their kind, for they are too nimble and watchful to be easily caught in the open, but the instincts of the nursery still live in their minds and so, when one calls, the others run to him if they cannot see him. If, as now, they can see him and he is not under threat, they merely watch him, wondering why he is calling. But at length one

of them moves. The lost one hears him and looking up, sees them. Happy again, he trots to the tree trunk and climbs up after them and the three play again, chasing each other through the branches.

They are tired now. It is still too early to seek the permanent shelter of their den, but they take a snooze in the pine. One hangs limply over a thick branch, head dangling towards ground, body precariously balanced on the timber; another is curled on a forked limb, seemingly comfortable; the third hangs like a half-empty sack on a thin limb high up the tree, his head on one side, most of his hindquarters on the other, one back foot finding toe-hold on a neighbouring branch. They sleep, inert bundles without a care, while the music of the bush night furnishes a lullaby; while, almost at the very foot of their tree, two little creatures are engaging in a strange ritual.

The salamanders remained in hiding under the damp, rotting leaves while the raccoons were gambolling around them; and it is well that they did, for the trio in the tree would have quickly eaten them. But now the danger is passed, at least for the time being, and these two are about to mate.

The two amphibians are about six inches long, dull olive green on the upper parts of their bodies, green and bluish speckled on the flanks and bellies, common enough creatures in Canada and the US. But seen here during this forest night, imagination could give them size and girth and transport them to the age of the giant creatures that haunted earth in the times of prehistory. Jefferson salamanders, they are called, and they live in the woodlands near swamps and streams and marshes, preying on insects and eating also of vegetable.

Now they are about to mate, a strange ritual in this act of life! The male, distinguished by his larger size, approaches the female and climbs upon her back, clasping her about the neck with his tiny, soft hands and arms. Then he pulls his body forward, so that he can rub her nose with the underside of his chin. They spend perhaps a minute thus. Now the male dismounts in front of her, keeping his back to her, and he strains his flanks and seems to be trying

to lay an egg. At last a small, moist sack emerges from his body. It is a bag of sperm. Now the male moves to one side, eyeing his sperm sack, upon which the female has advanced. She picks it up in her mouth and bends her body into a hoop, and after some gentle positioning, inserts this little bag into her rectal cavity, inside of which the bag bursts, releasing the captive male sperm which swim with their microscopic tails towards her womb, there to fertilize her waiting eggs. Now the ritual is ended, male and female move sluggishly amongst the decaying leaves and rotting wood, the male going about his own pleasures, the female seeking a suitable place upon which to lay her eggs. Both fade into the night, going into hiding within their world of dampness and rot.

On the other side of the lake, a great horned owl hoots mournfully. His cry awakens the raccoons. In unison they move, hoisting their bodies back on to the branches. They stretch, long and lazily and luxuriously, and then the big fellow begins to make his way down the tree. Head first he goes, his back feet swivelling easily to grip the nearly-smooth bark with the sharp claws, the pads of his front feet flat against the tree, taking the weight and acting as brakes, for he does not use these claws, but allows the pulpy pads to drag on the bark. In a moment he is down, and he must pause to scratch a flea pestering his right shoulder. The other two come down back-feet first, scrabbling along noisily, hanging on with their front paws, this time using the claws.

On the ground the three immediately begin to wrestle, but as quickly they stop when the deep call of owl reaches them again. They fade into the underbrush, infinitely quiet now, shadows of the night evading their greatest enemy. But they are safe as they go, for the owl is some distance away and has not seen them. And one, the smallest, stops to move his bowels, straining mightily, for the diet of insects is binding and he has not yet learned to purge himself by eating of the grasses.

An hour later, the three are full to repletion and they turn for home, an old marmot burrow, the entrance of which is under a cluster of granite rocks. Here they were born, here their mother

left them when she deserted them for her new mate. Here they will sleep safely during this year and go to ground when the deep cold comes. Then, next February, each will awake, body wasted and mating instincts aroused, and each will go his way, a rival to his brothers. Perhaps they will fight over some winsome female and from that time onwards they will greet each other warily, occasionally, mayhap, pausing for a brief greeting, then each going in an opposite direction, for they will be fully adult male raccoons, powerful creatures of quickness and endurance surprising in bodies that appear so cumbersome.

Tonight, though, as they bound along and stop now and then for a quick tussle. They are affectionate towards each other, three wild 'teenagers' of the forest, full of the zest for living, and if they still reek of skunk spray, none of them seems to mind, though their passage through the forest will remain marked by the skunk odour for at least twenty-four hours.

When they reach their den the moon is waning, the night is preparing to give way to the dawn. The owl hoots for several moments, then lifts its great wings and slides into air, steering a course for home. In the far distance a timber wolf howls and sudden silence descends on the lake and the forest. When no more wolf calls come, the frogs and toads begin again their incessant serenade and a whip-poor-will joins them, launching its monotonous call again and again, receiving answers from others like it. Crouched in the safety of a jumble of rocks, a white-footed mouse tries his small shrill voice also, a tiny soloist singing for his own pleasure, his reedy little voice almost drowned by the frogs.

A breeze has come and it plucks at the tree tops, making a new music. This is a deep sigh that now engulfs the area, a sigh punctuated now and then by the quick cracking of a dry limb that has been snapped off by the wind. Following the crack comes the sound of the fall, a swift, swishing, crackling noise that marks the passage of the fallen one through the restraining arms of its parent. Already the blueness of pre-dawn is creeping into the sky and some of the birds are responding to it, too sleepy yet to do more

than shuffle slightly on their perches, heads still tucked under one wing, while they chirp softly, their voices muffled by the feathers that hide the beaks. In another hour it will be dawn, a new day in a new month, for June is about to be born.

NINE

ONE MORNING in early June I took my red canoe down to the lake and set off on an aimless journey of exploration. The blackflies had eased a little and, although it was still early in the day, a scorching sun had banished most of the mosquitoes. A cheap cigar with which I punished myself and the flies, plus a liberal coating of 'Off,' kept my lightly-clad body comparatively safe from the bloodsuckers. I would collect a few bites and stings on this trip, but they would matter not, for the day was one for rejoicing, one of those robust, sun-filled dawning which are capable of steeping a man's mind and body with the excitement of just plain living.

Before me was the lake and its countless mysteries; above me the blue sky with its burning sun, around me the wilderness, and the birds, and the animals, and the insects. The day song of the forest was vibrant, the colours flashingly endless. In the reeds the voices of the geese and the ducks, lazily gentle; in the air the bursting songs of the birds, the buzzing of the flies, the rustling murmur of dragonfly wings, the sound of fresh green leaves rubbing against each other. The summer murmured constantly that day, it beckoned, promising new emotions, experiences hitherto unfelt, sights never before beheld. I cast off, pushing gently with my paddle against the granite of my launching place, letting the light canoe drift at will until it became time for a new, slow stroke.

At first I simply knelt relaxed in the canoe, soaking up the day, my mind freed of the problems of civilization and romping on its own through time and the past, my eyes watching whatever caught their fancy. As is usual with me on such occasions, I was at complete peace with myself and the world around me, a man-animal alone in his original setting, too busy observing to feel the need for companionship; indeed, not wanting the society of my kind, preferring this gentle loneliness that allowed me to listen to

my own thoughts and plucked responsive chords from my mind. Let me try and recapture that journey for you...

The smell of the wilderness. The admixture of a thousand odours blending as one to create freedom. The brownish waters highlighted by the sun giving off myriad reflections, allowing clear sight of the loam-brown lake bottom and of small things floating above it; a leech drifting by in aimless wriggle, seeking a creature upon which to fasten its sucker-mouth; a school of minnows undulating lazily six inches below the surface; the trailing stems of the lilies, the wet green of their floating leaves, the purity of the blooms. Here a sunken log, bloated with moisture, clustered with water growth, alive with the wriggle of minute animal life, one end anchored by the bottom mud, the other canted towards the surface, but no longer able to break clear.

Ahead, a seemingly endless stretch of thin lake decorated with the green and yellow and white of the lilies, its flat surface broken by the dormant bodies of fallen logs, ringed by granite that is splashed by the light greens and silvers of lichens. Beyond, the tall forest: the pines, the poplars, the maples, around which the birds flit and spiral and dart.

Now close by: on a lily pad a leopard frog sunning himself; a small frog, perhaps two inches long, looking cool and carefree as it waits for a fly upon which to breakfast. Nearby, a yellow brandy bottle upon the edge of which sits a dragonfly, fine legs gripping the golden petal, veined wings still, reflecting the sun, the green body shimmering the colours of the emerald. On the right gunwale of the canoe are two deer flies, coupled together in the mating act, their arrow-shaped bodies teetering unsteadily, the rustle of their wings a whisper of sound.

The canoe ripples gently through the water, the reeds and lily pads through which it is travelling shishing gently against the smooth sides, the only sound of our travel. Behind us, the slight wake tumbles its rolling course, like a panful of gently-boiling syrup atop the stove, beginning quite narrow, fanning outwards on its route towards the lake's shores, its movement bringing up

Wetlands are one of the most productive habitats on the planet. As more and more are being drained, we are not only losing amphibians like this frog that lives there, we are losing the trapped energy from the sun.

An American toad, another victim of disappearing wetlands, returns to its birthplace in the spring.

little particles of flotsam: bits of broken leaves, small, rotting twigs, the chitinous empty casing of a water beetle, another leech, a two-inch sack of tough muscle that now wriggles helplessly as it performs unwilling acrobatics at command of the current. Suddenly, a brownish shape detaches itself from the opening, fins arched like sails, showing the spiny ribs: a final lunge, the twist of the tail fluke, a small splash; the leech is gone. The bass swims down, leaving now a fast-spreading circle in the centre of the canoe-wake, two feet away from the stern.

Already heat haze is forming above the water. It dances and shimmers in the distance, projecting occasionally small mirages of water magically suspended in the air, somehow accentuating the shine of the sun on the broad pads of the distant lilies, distorting the shapes of insects as they fly through it, an impish curtain of unwanted sun-energy attempting to return to its birthright in far space. Then, seeming to materialize out of the heat haze, the sleek head of a beaver breaks water two hundred yards ahead of our prow, his arrival announced by a slight heaving of the water surface immediately above the place where his head appeared.

The beaver is casual. He has come up for a curious look at his world, he will eat a little, swim lazily on the surface, broad paddle-tail trailing limply behind his brownish body. And then if the bush-spirits move him, he may submerge and return to his lodge, or he may decide to inspect his dam; at this moment there is no telling what he will do with himself this day. Now he shows curiosity in the canoe. Unhurriedly, he makes a clean turn in the water, his bulk making not a sound as he steers with webbed back feet. He swims a wide circle around us, always keeping his head facing us. Three times he does this, inspecting the fat red thing that had invaded his world. He seems satisfied and he turns lazily for the north end of the lake and we watch the dark blob of his head as it becomes smaller and finally disappears from view.

Now a vulture sweeps overhead, an obscene bird if judged by the standards of human hygiene, a wonderful master of the air when seen like this; a great bird that spans six feet with its wings.

It is perhaps two hundred feet above, spiralling gracefully on still wings, the tips of which, like spread black fingers, vibrate gently as the gliding wings search out the updrafts and take advantage of them, while the spread tail steers. Tireless and patient is this bird with the red, featherless, wrinkled head, the quicksilver eyes, the broad, sensitive nostrils. We can see it turn, the crimson head moving, to left to right, a constant movement as it searches the ground and the water for carrion. And the birds of day leave it undisturbed, for this creature who lives on death does not kill, and the birds know this.

Near the canoe again. Crossing our bow is a sinuous chocolate-brown snake, a creature of graceful movement as it undulates its thirty-inch body on top of the water. It is a common water snake, dressed in two-toned brown, irregular markings, chocolate above, "café au lait" on the undersides. It is harmless to us, dangerous to the frogs and small fish of the lake. We watch it as it slithers on top of a lily leaf, pauses there a moment and slithers off again, only to submerge itself as it quests for prey.

In the shallows, hidden amongst the reeds, there are ducklings. Mallards, and black ducks, and wood ducks, and this year two families of horned grebes and one pair of Canada geese have stayed here. Now we can hear the peeping of the ducklings and we occasionally catch sight of the bright yellow-brown of their bodies, as they swim through their home sites. Once we come too close to the nest of the goose and the handsome, vigorous gander comes at us, neck stretched low, beak open, his voice at once a cry of warning to his mate and a threat to us. At once bedlam bursts upon the lake as all the ducks echo the gander's warning of intrusion and a nesting great blue heron flaps up from a quiet backwater nearby and climbs to the sky, scolding us with her hoarse voice. I paddle a little faster for we do not wish to disturb these creatures and, as we glide away, quiet returns and the birds continue feeding and 'talking' softly to each other.

Somewhere ahead, concealed in a marsh of catkins, a bittern calls its strange, pumping cry: oonk-a-woonk oonk-a-woonk

oonk-a-woonk. Then it is quiet, but the echo of its call has hardly become lost when the shrill cackle of a flicker replaces it; loud, long, rising above the voices of the marsh birds, seeming to stimulate the blackbirds to greater effort, for they increase the tempo of their songs as they prospect the lake in search of food.

We pause in our paddling to look back. Our wake loses itself behind us, but the passage of the canoe through the lilies is still noticeable, for the big leaves have not yet closed over the channel we have opened. Perhaps two hundred yards away a mallard duck is crossing the lake, leading a brood of seven ducklings, the little ones flanking her in arrow formation, peeping loudly, looking self-important as they follow their mother. One of the them breaks away and clambers on a partly-submerged log and runs along its length, a little bit of fluff obeying the whim of the moment.

We turn and paddle on, towards the spillway of the second beaver dam, and we see a brown muskrat slither into the water, hear the faint plop as he submerges. He was feeding on a small raft of cut catkin stems, platforms which these creatures make and leave scattered over the lake. Now the only sign of the rat is a stream of bubbles.

The sights and sounds and smells of this day are endless. They combine to capture the mood of early summer in the wilderness. Yet all is not as peaceful as our journey would indicate, as we shall see…

SUNSHINE AND GENTLE WIND, the lake and the forest, and the pleasant heat of an early June; for man in his idyll, a quiet, peaceful day inducing thoughts poetic in the mind. Can death come to spoil this scene? Indeed it can! And there it comes, carried by a lazy black dot spiralling through the sky half-a-mile above the lake and the forest.

The red-shouldered hawk has not killed today. All morning it spent quartering the forest in the area of its nest, flying mostly at tree-top height, occasionally coming lower to glide swiftly through the branches, constantly searching the ground and the trees for squirrel or chipmunk. But all eluded him, forcing him higher into the sky, so that his field of vision would be greater, increasing the span of his circles and taking him towards the lake, flying at unaccustomed altitude in the hope of securing prey which he must take to the poplar tree. There his bulky nest of sticks squats poised, housing three downy-white eyases and their mother, who now perches expectantly on the side of the nest. The hawk must kill, for there is need of meat in his eyrie. He "will" kill, for sooner or later he almost always does. And, like all the predators of the wilderness, he will kill quickly and he will kill well.

Now he is coming down and his proportions and colour change. He is no longer a dot, but shows the sleek outlines of a bird of prey; he is no longer dark, but instead presents his chest of rufus bars and the light underwings showing the white 'windows.' At once, the watchful blackbirds give the alarm. The purple grackles take it up and for a space of perhaps three seconds the air around the lake is shrill with the voices of the birds, each calling the warning. Then there is a bursting of feathered bodies as each species seeks cover in tree or shrub. And then there is silence and no movement, only the lazily-circling hawk up there.

Three times the hawk flies over the lake, his broad, stubby wings beating slowly, his short tail steering the chunky body. Now he alters course for the trees, where he is more at home, and soon he sees the movement of an unwary red squirrel as it is bounding along the forest floor, small limbs stiff, plumed tail carried upright.

The broad wings above are folded. The hawk dives. Too late the squirrel realizes his danger and tries to reach a tree. Inches from it, the talons of the hawk close on his body and the two crash heavily to the ground. Quickly the hawk strikes with curved beak and the blow almost severs the squirrel's head. In another instant the hawk is again airborne. He dodges through the trees, making for home, the limp body of the squirrel clutched in his talons.

Thus death came to the area of the lake, interrupting the peace and the thoughts of poetry in the mind of man; but not for long. Quickly the scene of peace returned on the heels of the kill and man was again free to pursue his lofty thinking. And this is irony, for peace is an empty, meaningless word in a wilderness which is "forever" in a state of war, and the human who would question the need for death here might just as well question the wisdom of his own particular God.

Nowadays, I am very conscious of the feelings of hatred which many well-intentioned people bestow upon the more obvious killers of the wild. These people pity the victims and loathe the wolf, and the bear, and the fox, and the hawk, and the cougar and the lynx. These and others who kill are the villains of Creation, the companions of the Satan of mythology, the symbols of evil. Feeling thus, these people will pause to admire the blue jay, or the thrush, or the robin; they will keep pretty goldfish and spend endless hours admiring these gentle creatures. And they will not know (or will not admit) that these things of physical beauty, of gorgeous song, are themselves ruthless killers.

Take the dove, symbol of peace upon this universe. What happens if two male doves are placed in a cage and begin to fight (as they would inevitably do)? If man does not rescue the loser, the victor will peck him to a bloody pulp, viciously and unmercifully. Ugly? Yes, by the standards of civilization. But real, very real. And simple, for primitive death is always accompanied by a simple lethal act. Only man contrives exquisite refinements with which to encompass the ghastly sadism of unnecessary killing. Man, the arch predator, the most ruthless, vicious animal of them all. Slowly and painfully the man-animal evolved, from a primitive creature who killed when his belly was empty to a sophisticate of high intellect who hires his butcher and daintily gnaws upon the meat of his victims while giving up his mind to thoughts lofty and inspirational.

He talks of peace and is ever a long way from achieving it. Perhaps when he will achieve it, he will then understand the workings of Creation, of God. But in the meantime, by getting to know the wilderness, by recognizing that life is premised on death, that there are those that kill and those that are killed, man may learn to come to terms with himself. It has been thus with me. The wilderness has taught me many things, but the most important of them all is the realization that life is a precious, delicate substance. And although I am still a meat-eater, and therefore guilty of killing 'by proxy,' life, any life, has never been of more value to me than it is today.

Thinking about life and about my reluctance to take it, I asked myself recently: What is it about a living being that is so full of fascination for me? There is one major element of life that perhaps could qualify, in part, at least, as an answer: the painfully-long, marvellously-intricate process of evolution. If the history of modern civilization begins with the Renaissance or the Middle Ages, then the two most important biological events ever to have occurred on earth took place during the Silurian Period, which began 425 million years ago and lasted for 50 million years; frightening enormities of time during which the limitless patience of Creation made and tested and discarded and, inch by slow inch, eventually whelped air-breathing animals and grew the first land plants.

It is true that these things of life that escaped the waters of prehistory were rude and primitive, compared with the refinements which Creation was to incorporate into them later, but they marked the start. The plants were giant fern-life fronds that dominated the land scene for the next 100 million years; the air-breathing animals were arachnids, creatures resembling modern scorpions, after which modern man named the spiders and scorpions and similar insects. But why did Creation begin land life with these two particular species? And here is another direct question to which there is no simple answer. We can only accept the fact that this is what happened, for fossil and other evolutionary evidence tells us so, but whether this was nature's first choice, or merely the last and most effective experiment during countless ages of trial and error we shall never know. It is enough to realize that the combination, no matter how it was brought about, was the right one, as we shall see…

Through each age and period that was to follow, right to the present day, plants and insects kept step with each other's evolution.

It is significant to note here that, in the absence of man, the relationships between the insects and the flowering plants have always been friendly, a system of mutual co-operation which has persisted from prehistory to modern times. Plants afford food and shelter to the insects and in their turn insects become the 'midwives' of the plants, cross-pollinating the flowers, ensuring the union of male and female. In time, flowering plants developed certain colours and scents with which to attract their insect benefactors and, in turn, the insects developed physical characteristics of mouth and body which would enable them to feed off the plants and at the same time provide the service of elementary life. Eventually, the two groups became interdependent to the point that now, if our insects were to be wiped out, countless numbers of plants and shrubs and trees would perish, and likewise, if the plants were to die, the insects would die with them.

Naturally, in order to create those early plants and insects nature had to decide upon the raw materials she was to use for the process; and these were selected from amongst elements that had been formed when, out of the chaos of space, the planet earth took its place in the universal scheme. Then, as now, these elements provided 99 percent of the substance that characterized all living things. Only one fraction remained to be added: Life. It was (if I may be permitted a rather elementary analogy) as though a complex lighting circuit had been manufactured: the wiring had been installed, the bulbs made, the fuses inserted; then the switch was pulled, and life sprang through the system. But how this came about is still anybody's guess, though biologists today believe that the mystery of life can be explained in terms of physics and of chemistry and not through some unexplained vital force. Although these beliefs are but guesses, still they are educated ones, backed by a vast array of scientific research. Perhaps time may prove them right. Or wrong?

At any rate, we know today that five major elements furnish the basic ingredients of life during an equal number of cycles. The first of these is carbon, the second nitrogen, the third phosphorus, the fourth water and the fifth energy. With the aid of other elements which we shall meet later, these five combine to make matter, the semi-solid substance of which all things are made and which is used again and again, for according to science, matter is neither created or destroyed, but remains on earth forever. In fact, we are told that the total amount of animal and plant protoplasm that has ever existed since life first began on earth would, if added together, form a mass many times larger than our planet. And if, on death, the protoplasm of an animal was not re-used by earth and was allowed, instead, to lie around, in the billion or so years since life first began in the water so much of this dead matter would have accumulated on our planet that this would have swelled to many times its present size.

Fortunately this has not happened, for Creation is a careful housekeeper. Instead of wasting dead matter, it has provided organisms that thrive on it, breaking it down to its original components and returning it later to use. Thus, the carbon that is in use today is undoubtedly the same as the carbon that was in use, say, during the Silurian Period, when the arachnids and the land plants were formed. Careful scientific calculations show that there are some six tons of carbon (in the shape of carbon dioxide) floating in the air above each acre of the earth's entire surface. This amount remains constant, despite the fact that each year one acre of plants will take out of the atmosphere as many as twenty tons of carbon. This is explained simply. Obviously, if there are only six tons of carbon suspended over one acre of land, and if this were the only supply of the substance, the green plants of earth would use up all the atmosphere's supplies of carbon in space of about thirty-five years. And there are other creatures, too, that use the substance. But there is no great mystery about all this. In the first place, carbon is only *borrowed* for a time, to circulate through the bodies of plants and animals and then to be exhaled in the form of carbon dioxide back into the atmosphere. In the second place, both the decay bacteria that attacks all dead tissue and the fungi which grow upon the bodies of various types of dead things extract carbon from their lifeless hosts, through the processes of putrefaction and of fermentation. Thus, this carbon is turned it into carbon dioxide which returns to the atmosphere, there to be used again.

A similar cycle controls the use and re-use of nitrogen, the second vital substance of life which makes up almost 80 percent of the earth's atmosphere and which is needed by plants and all animals for the manufacture of body substance (protoplasm).

Despite the fact that it is available in such large quantities in the air, this essential gas can only become converted into usable chemical salts by some algae and by bacteria that grow in the soil. A third group of bacteria which is unable to extract nitrogen gas from the air on its own, combines with certain cells in the roots of some plants (the legumes, to which family peas and beans belong) and with their assistance extracts the gas from the air and changes it into chemical salts. These few plants and the soil bacteria are responsible for supplying the earth with the chemical salts of nitrogen so essential to life. Indeed, the algae, the plants and the bacteria can be said to be 'farmers' of nitrogen which they store in the soil, from where it is taken as needed by the green plants which absorb the salts (nitrates) through their roots, and then convert them into the acids and proteins of protoplasm.

By eating the plants, animals absorb the vegetable acids and use them to make their own protoplasm. And, because many species of animals who eat only green plants absorb more nitrogen salts than their bodies can use, they return the unwanted supplies to the soil with their body wastes, which are immediately attacked by the soil bacteria and converted into ammonia. This is then used by two different kinds of soil bacteria during two more operations, the last of which is responsible for salvaging the nitrogen salts from the ammonia and putting them back into the earth for the use of the plants, thus completing the cycle. But in the meantime, in order to ensure that life and time do not drain all the nitrogen gas from the atmosphere, another form of bacteria, the denitrifying bacteria, convert some of the ammonia into atmospheric nitrogen and release this from the earth into the atmosphere. Likewise, when animals and plants die, the decay

bacteria convert the nitrogen compounds left in their bodies into ammonia, which is also converted into nitrogen salts or denitrified into atmospheric nitrogen.

The third substance of life is phosphorus; and an important one it is, too, for it is essential to the making of body-matter, and although its cycle is not as finely-balanced as those of carbon and nitrogen (for much of it is carried off to the sea bottom, from where it returns haphazardly), still it is absorbed by plants and animals, kept by them for a time, and then returned to the earth or to the water for reuse.

The phosphorus cycle is relatively simple. The substance is found in the rocks of the earth and is taken from them by the action of water, which wears their surfaces and washes out various minerals from them. Among these is phosphorus, which is converted into phosphates by plants and animals, the first from the water and the soil, the second from the water they drink and the food they eat, and it is returned to the soil and to the water when they die. Meanwhile, some of unused phosphorus is carried away by streams and rivers into the sea, where it sinks to the bottom. Some of it is absorbed by fish (freshwater fish, of course, also absorb it from the lakes and rivers) and some of these fish are eaten by seabirds, and by man, and the phosphates of their bodies are returned for earthly use. At various times, upheavals of the sea bottom return to the surface some of the phosphorus that has stayed there and this, too, becomes available on earth, which is fortunate, for the substance is carried into the seas faster than it is normally returned by them.

The fourth vital 'food' is water, which needs little more explanation here. It is, as I have said, absolutely essential to all life, not only because our bodies require it, but because it co-operates with the other four cycles of life in the storage and distribution and growth of all other substances and organisms. And yet, carbon and nitrogen and phosphorus and water would be useless without the last substance: energy, the only important source of which is the sunlight that reaches earth, which is released by atomic explosions that occur at unimaginably-high temperatures in the bowels of the sun, which will, eventually, exhaust all its fuel. When that happens, all life will perish on earth, but, science tells us, we do not have to worry just now, for the sun's death is not expected to take place for several billions of years yet!

Only a small proportion of the sun's energy that reaches earth is 'trapped' for our use. Plants do this, using it through photosynthesis to store it in their bodies to be used as it is needed to provide fuel to drive the complex chemical reactions that occur in all living things. When animals eat plants, the substances of the plant that have trapped and stored this energy oxidize within the animal, and the energy is thus freed and becomes available to drive the animal's 'motor.' When a plant-eating animal is eaten by a predator, the energy of its body passes into the body of the predator. Thus the cycle of energy goes. But not all the trapped energy is used by those that consume it, for whenever energy is transferred from one thing to another, it loses some of its 'driving force,' which escapes into outer space in the form of heat, so that eventually, all the sun energy that is trapped by plants is converted into heat and lost. That is why fresh supplies from the sun are constantly needed.

Now, although the five cycles mentioned can be classed as the major elements of life, all living things require many other chemicals in order to function—to "live." Principally, carbon, oxygen, hydrogen and nitrogen make up almost 96 percent of the body; while calcium, phosphorus, potassium and sulphur make up another 3 percent. The remaining 1 percent is made up of tiny quantities of iodine, iron, sodium, magnesium, chlorine, manganese, copper, zinc and cobalt, and the chances are that minute proportions of a few other chemicals also are needed.

All these chemical elements combine through fantastically complex and numerous series of reactions to form 'Life,' which began humbly after it had been spawned in the seas of prehistory more than one billion years ago. Is it any wonder, then, that I find myself loath to destroy something so incredibly ancient and intricate? In a split second man can take a life: it is all too easy!

But despite the wonders of our progress and the intricacies of our scientific achievements, we are still unable to make life (other than by following the percepts of "natural" procreation) and we do not even really know what it is. And, whereas I would feel no compunctions about killing if my survival depended upon it (for, after all, this is the law of Creation), the unnecessary slaughter of animals or plants, or even insects, has now become abhorrent to me.

I do not condemn the hunting man, for he is merely obeying deeply-buried instincts which are yet still active within him. Once he had to be a predator in order to survive. Today, while he is still carnivorous, his intelligence has shown him how to obtain his food without hunting it. Although this is still a kind of predation, it sets man apart from the prowling hunters of the wilderness; so much so, in fact, that he would no longer be able to survive in the state of wild if he were to find himself transported there, stark naked and deprived of all the essentials of civilized living. Then he would be the weakest, most defenseless creature of all. He would quickly perish from cold in winter and from the ravages of insects in the summer. The only weapons available to him then would be fallen tree branches and stones and possibly, if he had the wit to survive that long and had gathered previously the practical knowledge, he might be capable of making a primitive, stone-tipped spear, or a bow and some arrows. But I doubt that he would live long enough to fashion these instruments! Perhaps in some areas of this earth, those of moderate clime, he would survive to rise again as king animal driven by his intelligence, but in the forests of North America the elements would defeat him long before he could harness his wits. Personally, I do not propose to attempt such an experiment. Well supplied with the necessary clothing, I just might consider giving it a try one of these days. But *naked*? I shudder at the thought!

ON AGAIN NOW, pushing the canoe towards the marsh area, gliding smoothly and with no more sound than that of the murmuring ripple of the canvas against the water, the occasional music of

droplets falling from the broad blade of the paddle. And it is the water itself that draws us as we float upon it and hear its whispered movement; the water without which life could not be. And we watch as one glistening drop forms on the edge of the paddle, elongates itself into a drip and tumbles downwards to splash back into the lake with a power surprising in such a tiny bubble of moisture.

Above us the sky is still clear, but that drop that we watched reminds us of rain, of the force of rain, and of the quantity of rain which falls on the American continent during the course of one year. And which, if it fell all at one time, would inundate our entire land mass with two-and-a-half feet of water. We are reminded, too, that there are many kinds of rain: rain that is fat, but gentle; rain that is thin and constant; rain that is gross and savage; rain that is regular and *wetting*, that falls controlled and soaks slowly into the earth and flows through the streams and rivers, and into the ponds and pools and lakes and eventually returns to the seas.

It is the rain that has made this lake and now continues to nurse it with the help of the beaver. It is the rain that brings all the various kinds of animals and birds and insects to this section of my wilderness; that grows the trees and shrubs and wild flowers. And here each and every drop of rain that falls upon the earth travels the last portion of its descent slowly, striking the leaves of the trees, or the blades of the grasses, or the heads of the mushrooms, shattering into smaller particles that slip off the obstacles their parents have encountered and quietly soak into the soil on the first stage of their return trip to the oceans. These clean crystals of moisture have been sucked up by the sun, tumbled across the heavens and released over this place; clean crystals of moisture that remain clean as they soak into the soil. There is nothing here to mar their purity and they are allowed to travel their careful course through the dead vegetation that is already being 'farmed' by soil bacteria and to continue on down, through top soil, there to be seized by the thirsty roots of the plants that grow in this earth, interrupting their journey for a time while they give life to the forest.

By canoe. No better way to explore the countless mysteries of the lake.

Here, in this wilderness, the rain is always a friend. It may rush in, boisterously virile, or it may slip down quietly, but it comes as an ally to the wilderness. How different these same drops that strike the bare earth of a carelessly planned farm field! Then, each drop becomes a small fury, a tiny bomb that smashes with amazing force at the defenceless topsoil and sends it flying upwards in minute spurts that return to a new place. A heavy downpour on such land washes away the soil of ages, carrying it along the valleys of the straight furrows, to deposit it useless in some ditch and eventually wash it down to the bottom of streams and rivers and lakes, stealing it. How different, too, this clean rain when it falls into some lake or river that has been fouled by the unclean wastes of man! Then it becomes wasted, of no use to the earth, its bulk giving greater volume to the poisons that have been so carelessly allowed to accumulate; poisons which rob the water of its oxygen and which make the water opaque, shutting out the sunlight from the bottom, robbing energy from the few organisms that are still trying to survive.

Here, upon this wild, free lake, there is health. Beyond the trees at our back, in the southlands where scurrying humans mill like so many ants upon a hill, there is sickness. Water sickness, a slowly-spreading, inexorable disaster that is killing, one by one, the rivers and the streams and the lakes of Continental America. Desperately, a few men and women are trying to halt its spread; carelessly, a vast multitude is busy broadcasting it. And compounding the disease, water that is not contaminated by it is robbed of its resting place as more and more land becomes invaded by bulldozers, levelled for the construction of houses and factories; drained for agriculture, so that more food can be grown to feed more men and women. And, they, through their issue, require the robbing of more land for housing space and factory site and farm. A slow circle this, but a vicious one, which, in the United States alone, has so far claimed some one billion acres of earth and has poisoned countless waterways, while in Canada, this lusty, sprawling giant of a land, it is inexorably moving forward, through few figures are available with which to compute its ravages. But this wilderness of mine is still unspoiled, and I shall fight to keep it so.

Here, at this very spot where we now float in the canoe, where the muskrat marsh begins hesitatingly to join the lake, there is to be found the health and vigour of a flourishing wilderness, so perhaps we should not now think of those ailing places so far to the south of us. Let us instead turn the bow of the canoe and glide into the marsh, past the derelict body of a downed pine, and into the beaver and muskrat channels that wind carelessly between the busbied catkins. And let us pause here, and question the marsh, which was once a lake in its own right and has been painstakingly built up through the ages into a place of shallow water and abundance of organic matter that one day will become a swamp. A place where new trees will root, and grow, and die, and fall down, and with their bodies provide more organic matter that one day, long after you who read this, and I who am writing, are gone, will be converted into soil, for this is the cycle of the wilderness. Where there is water today, there will be land tomorrow; where there was land yesterday, there is water today. This is the way of the good

farmer; the rotation of crops, the conditioning of plant life and animal life. The changes must be made well, and at the right time; they must not be rushed, they must not be poorly effected.

Ahead of us a strange shape scuttling over a rock flat, moving towards the marsh. A muskrat has been disturbed and is escaping, his small feet moving so quickly that the creature would seem to be rolling forward upon a set of invisible wheels. His short front legs cause his chest and shoulders and head to be held low to the ground, his long back legs raise his haunches, giving him a hunch-backed look, showing him clumsy on land. But he reaches the water and is at once transformed into a sleek, agile creature that dives gracefully and swims as easily as a fish. We watch him for a moment, then he is gone, leaving the trail of small bubbles that have escaped his fur and his nostrils.

Near us, busy on a fluffed-out catkin, a hornet is eating a botfly. The predator sits on its downy platform and holds the captive fly with its forelegs, its jaws busy. The fly's wings have already been removed, now the hornet's jaws pull bits from the fly, which is still alive and trying feebly to escape. The hornet twirls it as though it were a tiny cob of corn. In a few moments it has eaten all but the fly's head and this it drops, whether by design or because it has slipped through its clutching legs, we do not know. Now the big insect preens itself, seeming to enjoy the warmth of the day. In another moment it has gone, disturbing a few shreds of the catkins down which now float slowly towards the water.

We are about to push on into the maze of catkins, but a slight rustling amongst them draws our attention. At first we cannot see beyond the miniature forest of stems, but suddenly the tiny body of a brownish bird appears for an instant between two stems. It is a marsh wren, a perky little bird that carries its short tail erect, whose longish legs seem to emerge from the very end of its chunky body and who constantly stoops forward. Now we can see that its brownness is broken by patterns of black stripes and there is a small whiteness on its breast. It is unafraid, disappearing amongst the catkins only to appear again, perched on a leaning

stem, fixing us with one beady eye. As though in greeting, it sings a reedy little song that somehow manages to gurgle and ends in a long guttural rattle. Then it is gone. As we move away, we hear the quiet rustle of its passage amongst the catkins.

Soon we must turn and retrace our course, for the marsh is falling away now and there is scarcely floating room, even for the shallow craft that we are paddling. But there is still the return journey to look forward to, and new sights will greet us along it. The day is older, there are a few milk clouds in the sky; more birds sing as we manoeuvre the canoe, turning it within the confinement of the marsh and its catkins.

Concealed by the forest, a pileated woodpecker smashes at a standing tree, his steel-hard bill probing for the insects that he knows hide within. The cackle of a flicker rises above the pileated's powerful drumming, mingling with the constant whistles of the red-winged blackbirds and the rusty creaking of the grackles. We hear a hawk's call, but we cannot see the bird and we know by the faintness of its cry that it is some distance away, perhaps circling around the area of the cabin. And then we are turned and we dip the yellow paddles and push the canoe southwards, still going quietly and slowly, pausing often to study some part of this lake of mine, in no hurry to leave it. The day is good.

EVENING. The sun still glows crimson against the western trees, its light silhouetting the small new leaves of the poplars and elms and maples, making stark the angled lines of the evergreens. We walk the trail that leads to home, to the cabin perched inside the ring of green pines where Joan readies our supper. It has been a long day of wonder and calm and, for us, peace. Now we are tired and very hungry. The bites of the flies are beginning to burn and itch a little, for our bodies have sweated and our perspiration has washed away the 'Off' in some places, and the bloodsuckers found these and drank from us. But they are welcome, for how can we compare the value of the few drops of blood that we have lost against the wealth of pleasure and experience that my lake has

given us this day? And even the bloodsuckers repay us for their food. Hear them now as they sing, joining the chorus of the frogs and the toads that signals the start of another night.

We pause a moment and look back. The vague, long shape nestling under a bushy balsam fir is the canoe, its colour lost in shadow. A sparkle or two winks at us from the surface of the lake. A nighthawk voices its nasal cry, then booms noisily as it emerges from a steep dive. Clear upon the darkening forest rings the chant of the whip-poor-will.

TEN

SUMMER AT MY LAKE. The voices and colours of the birds; the bustle of their activity as they raise their young. How many species of birds live in the area of my lake? I do not know, for I have never counted them, reserving this task for a time appropriate; this time, so that I may record them all here. And so that you, the reader of this book, may come with me and spend the rest of this summer beside the lake, observing and counting and classifying as many birds as we can find, studying their shapes and their habits and their voices and the food they eat...

DAWN IN JULY. In the east the rosy light of day creeping into the paleness of sky, rimming the distant trees, highlighting their shapes and creating dense shadows within the bulk of their branched bodies. On the wild grasses and shrubs there is dew, fresh and crystalline, spreading the sheen of wetness on blades and leaves, hanging hesitant on the spear-like tips of the grasses. Little globules of moisture trapping feeble sun-energy and reflecting the blue of sky and the green of trees and the warm tones of earth; miniature kaleidoscopes which are insignificant from a distance and become pure bubbles of colourful wonder when we stoop and peer at them closely. There, see that one? It is already pear-shaped and will fall to the earth soon, but now it glistens and shimmers and the colours of the rainbow live within it. A mite of a spider is sipping from it, a little red spider, hardly larger than the head of a pin. His web, lightly-sprayed by dew and no bigger than a copper penny, has been fastened to the stems of grass, low down, barely two inches above the soil, a gossamer little net shining silver in the weak light of this new day.

Reluctantly, we must leave the spider and the dew drop and the grass, for I have set up a blind on the small rock island that shelters the large beaver lodge. We must go there, paddling slowly in the canoe, and take our places within the sack-cloth shelter, for soon the bustle of birdlife will reach its peak. Already the songs of these creatures fill the air around us as we leave the shore and head for the blind: blackbirds, and grackles, and jays, and chickadees, and marsh wrens, and crows, and ducks and herons, and the bitterns; and a host of others. They all pour their songs upon the dawn, some sweetly melodious, others harsh, yet others shy, whispered melodies.

The slightly pungent smell of the sackcloth mixes with the sharp scent of the repellent we have sprayed upon ourselves; the odour of the lake comes to us also. In a few moments we shall become accustomed to these smells, now they are strong and not unpleasant, characteristics of the quest upon which we are intent. We sit silent, peering through the round holes cut in the sacking, watching the lake while we clutch notepad and pencil, ready to scribble the names of the creatures that we see, to record their behaviours...

The sky is reflected on lake water that is almost still, disturbed only by gentle ripples that come and go as unseen creatures and currents activate the lower stratas of liquid. Suddenly the placid water opposite the western window of the blind begins to erupt, rolling upwards sluggishly to form an evanescent liquid mound that is almost immediately replaced by the head and body of a smallish, chunky water bird that wears conspicuous golden 'horns' on both sides of its head. Between the horns the head and cheeks are black; atop the bird's back, the body feathers reflect a blue-black colour. A wide band of rufus feathers begins at the erect neck and travels down over the upper portions of its chest and along both sides of the body and, as the duck-like creature raises itself slightly in the water, the white breast is revealed. 'Horned grebe,' we write, and then, as five brownish-striped youngsters scuttle quickly into view, we note further: 'female with chicks.'

The mother drops something on the surface of the water and the fuzzy youngsters dash to it, each fighting for a share of the morsel which we are unable to recognize; it may be a leech, or a small fish, or a water beetle. The scramble ends. One chick holds his head up and the throat muscles work; it is swallowing the prize, while the mother bobs suddenly and dives, cleaving the water as she streaks away to seek more food for her brood. The chicks swim about aimlessly, attractive, agile little birds who await the female's return.

The young grebes look to be about three weeks old, which means that the eggs from which they emerged were laid by the female some seven weeks ago, for the young hatch in twenty-four or twenty-five days. Before that the courting ritual took place on the lake, both adult birds took part in a series of nuptial dances; treading water with their un-webbed feet, rising upright in the water to face each other and then to circle, face-to-face, while they shake their plumes and now and then touch beaks. Both birds look alike; both have the golden horns, patches of feathers that begin at the ruby eyes as narrow yellow bands and fan backwards and upwards to end in tousled horns. Now the horns are fully erected, gorgeous plumes which are shaken occasionally during the ceremony which must take place before the mating.

After that the eggs were laid. Five whitish ovals were deposited by the female within the cup of an untidy floating nest that was supported by a raft of mud and plant stems and anchored to the stems of catkins, and upon which, turn-and-turn-about, both birds sat constantly for almost four weeks.

After the youngsters were born, father and mother escorted their precocious brood over the lake, taking them amongst the catkins for shelter, herding the quick-moving, free-swimming chicks away from dangers, or keeping a watch while the brood swam carelessly upon open water. Then, as the chicks grew stronger and more able to take care of themselves, the father seemed to tire of parental duties. Gradually he moved away, each morning exploring farther from the nest area and staying away longer; at last he stayed away altogether and the mother continued alone to take care of her young.

This morning she is teaching them how to hunt, now and then breaking off her instruction to dive steeply and find some succulent bit of life for herself and for them, for undisciplined youngsters scare away more food then they can find, and the surface hunting has not been good this day. The chicks circle expectantly around another one of those gentle upheavals of water. Mother appears and now she is holding a large tadpole between her pointed mandibles; it is the tadpole of a bullfrog, alive and still wriggling feebly, a creature almost two inches long with a fat round body and a tapering tail. The mother drops it on the water. Again a scramble; the water boils as the little grebes fight for the food. One succeeds, pulls out of the melee swallowing frantically, not content until the fat pollywog is safely ensconced within the damp darkness of its gullet.

Suddenly, the mother bird looks up, uneasy about something. She remains still on the water and one of her youngsters climbs upon her back and disappears into a feathered 'pocket' between her wings. The grebe lets loose an ear-splitting screech. At once the water froths as the family races for the shelter of the catkins. What has disturbed them?

Coming in low and swiftly from the northern part of the lake, a 'blue hawk' quests for prey. He sees the grebes, but is too far away to drop on one of the chicks. But he keeps coming, skimming the tops of the catkins, forever searching, for this male marsh hawk has a mate and three eyases to feed. 'Marsh hawk, male,' we note as we watch.

The blue-grey head and back are visible as the bird passes the blind, veers swiftly to investigate something amongst the lily pads and then turns again towards the south. He is about eighteen inches long and has a wingspan of more than two feet, the ends of his primary feathers black. Showing clearly his 'fingers' spread, he glides by a second time and he disappears amongst the shrubs in the southeast. Still skimming low, his quick eyes searching, keen ears listening for the rustle of mouse, or mole, or duckling, while a quarter of a mile away, concealed by the thick shelter of a dwarf

juniper bush, the big female guards the four downy-white eyases, and waits for the sharp whistle of her mate to signal a kill.

These two were born on this lake several years ago. This spring they came here again from the southlands and, later, the male began his spectacular courting dives. Rising sixty or more feet above the forest, he would halt suddenly in mid-air, then his body would be launched towards the ground in a streaking dive. Seconds before the graceful bird smashed into the forest floor, a quick movement of the tail, a checking with the wings, and he pulled out easily, flapping his wings lazily and climbing the sky once more. Again and again he repeated these manoeuvres, tirelessly, effortlessly, while his brown-streaked mate alternately watched him from the ground and quested away on a short hunting circle of their domain. Now and then she would rise and join him in the aerobatics, after which she would return to the nest area and watch, or hunt, while he, indefatigable, continued to dive and climb, perhaps plummeting his sturdy body towards ground seventy or more times before he broke off to go hunting with his mate.

After the show-off time, the time of courting displays that characterizes all bird nuptials, the pair settled to the serious task of raising one more brood of hawks. Now the male busied himself gathering nesting materials which he would take to his mate. She would fashion these into a cup of nest, making a crude platform on the ground, under the overhanging, prickly branches of the juniper, further concealed by thick bushes that grew in the damp area near the big catkin marsh. And when the nest was done, the eggs were laid; four of them, blue-white and faintly splotched with brown. Both birds took turns at sitting, warming the eggs, turning them until, four weeks later, the downy youngsters chipped their way free and tottered feeble bodies within the cup. Unsteady legs were already trying to carry the weight of the white shapes and only succeeding in overbalancing their owners, so that the eyases were constantly falling against each other, raising their wobbly heads from under the downy bodies of their brothers and sisters.

Now the female stayed close to her nest while her mate har-
ried the area around the marsh and the lake, always hunting for
himself and his family, his wings alternately flapping and gliding,
forming a constantly-recurring V as he systematically quartered his
hunting territory. At sight of prey, the long fanned tail slams downwards suddenly, his progress brought to a jolting stop that immediately is followed by the killing plunge, black talons questing,
binocular eyes firmly fixed upon the prey. A quick stabbing thrust
of the talons, the prey is killed; a curving of the long claws, the
bird rises with the meat, emitting his shrill whistle. He flies higher now, angling towards the nest. The female sees him and rises
from the ground, streaking upwards. Suddenly, the male releases
his prey; it tumbles inertly towards the earth, but never reaches it,
for the female streaks at it and grasps it in mid-air. The male flies
off on another hunt, the female takes the kill to the young.

At first, when the hatchlings are still feeble, she rips the prey,
holding it with one powerful foot while her curved beak rends it.
A morsel at a time, she feeds each eyas, all of which become wild
in the scramble for the meat. Later, when they are bigger and have
acquired some of their strength and have developed enormous
appetites, the mother must also go out to hunt. Now both birds
stop by the nest with their kills, dropping a dead mouse or a
young bird amongst their offspring. Now the young hawks have
learned to tear the meat for themselves and each competes with
the others for the prey. As one seizes the food, he hunches over it,
mantling it with spread wings in an effort to keep it for himself.
But soon the kill is torn apart and each bird is busy stuffing pieces
of it down his throat; fur or feathers, meat and bone going down
into the crop, where the digestive juices of the youngsters will sort
out the indigestible portions from those that are needed to build
muscle and bone and sinew. Later, the fur and feathers and bits
of bone will be cast in the form of roundish pellets, some of
which will stay inside the nest and become part of it, others landing outside to disintegrate, in time, and become absorbed by the
forest floor.

While the parents are away, the eyases practise the hunting skills that one day will take them soaring through the air in chase of prey. At three weeks they begin to jump into the air, flapping their fledgling wings, exercising them for the time of flight. In another week or so they leave the nest and scramble about in the juniper, trying out their still-small powers in short, hopping flights, while the parent birds continue hunting and carrying back food for them to quarrel over. Now and then, when the adult birds have been away longer than usual, the young ones cry to them, ringing calls, high-pitched and shrill. These are the cries that now reach the male hawk as he skims over the catkins, clutching the body of a young muskrat. He heeds the calls, turning from his course and passing in front of the blind, flying level with it, and as he leaves we can clearly see the dangling rat, gripped tightly by those great black talons, two strings of blood marking twin red lines on the brown fur.

For a time the water is empty around the rock island. The droning of the flies mingles with the songs of the birds and the small rustling sounds made by the leaves of the aspens. Beyond our blind we can see the dragonflies and the damselflies as they quest the air for mosquitoes and blackflies, now and then pausing in their hunts to mate briefly in the air. The singing of the redwings is clear and melodious, the calls of the flickers loud, mingled with the occasional drumming of the woodpeckers' percussion noises of the forest.

Presently the quacking of ducks draws our attention to the water. Three mallard drakes swim into view, their colours not so prime now, for they are in the moult and will be unable to fly until all their new feathers have developed. They swim by and we note them in our log. And again empty water. But not for long. Now a brown, mottled female mallard leads her flotilla of yellow-brown babies, their peeping loud, rising above the soft quacking of the mother bird. They swim lazily around the island, now on this side, and as quickly, paddling around the rock and searching for food on the other side.

Mallards arrive early in the spring, and stay well into the autumn
before migrating south.

The wood duck drake, one of the most beautiful of our waterfowl.

They are sturdy birds, these mallards, coming early in spring and staying until the frosts of autumn clothe the lake in a thin sheet of ice. Even then, a few linger until the ice has become heavy and it requires too much effort to beat at it with their wings to keep a hole open. Then they rise and point south, to their wintering grounds along the Gulf Coast and the Mississippi Valley.

In the spring the courtship rituals of the drakes are long and elaborate, each bird following the same pattern, performing a complex water dance that, as far as can be established, has remained the same through the ages. And after the mating, within a nest of down and grasses concealed amongst the reeds, the duck lays eight to twelve eggs and patiently sits on them, until almost four weeks later the yellow and brown youngsters peck through the imprisoning shells. At this time the drakes are away, in-hiding amongst the reeds, shedding their beautiful breeding plumage, eclipsing their colours for softer, safer shades. Lakebound, squads of temporary bachelors gather and 'gossip' in their soft, somewhat squeaky voices, content to allow their ducks to raise the ducklings unaided.

Now the mother mallard is immediately opposite our blind, surrounded by her young, and we must have made some sound, some movement that has captured her attention. She issues a loud warning cry and her ducklings streak towards the shallows near our dock and dive, their fluffy bottoms upturning as they head for underwater concealment. If we were able to leave the blind and peer down, we would see them, nine little bundles whose outstretched necks and heads point upwards, beaks closed, round eyes open, immobile, anchored somehow to the bottom.

Atop the water, the mother swims back and forth anxiously for a moment or two; then she seems to accept the alien blind and begins to swim towards the place where her young ones have dived. Before she reaches it the little ones pop to the surface, buoyant as corks, apparently unconcerned now. The family moves away, the duck quacking, the small ones peeping. They make for the reeds, there to feed, or to rest, secure within the shelter they know so well.

A wood duck comes by; a drake, still preserving in his feathers the glories of the rainbow, but a little shabby now, for he, too, is in the moult. As we record his presence, he is joined by seven other drakes and the squadron passes beyond our vision, a cluster of wondrous birds, perhaps the most beautiful of nature's creatures. At the height of the breeding season, these magnificent drakes glow with irridescent hues which are accentuated by stripes of pure white: blue and green and bronze and ruby and yellow and mauve, an impossible array to capture upon paper, a sight capable of thrilling even the most unpoetic amongst us.

Unlike the mallards, who pick their mates in spring after their return migration flight, wood ducks pair off on their winter feeding grounds, and it is the female that leads the male back to the place of her choosing, perhaps the area in which she was born, or possibly she may select that part of the forest where she nested during the previous year. It is in one of these places that, after mating, she searches for a suitable nesting tree, perhaps the excavated burrow of a squirrel, thirty or forty or more feet up the bole of poplar or maple or elm, or it may be that she takes over the nesting hole of a pileated woodpecker. But whether squirrel den or woodpecker hole, the wood duck nests high above ground and in a tree, sitting on between ten and fifteen white eggs.

When her babies are born, they are faced with a seemingly impossible task: they must get out of their nest and reach the ground so far below them. And for a long time people have argued about the way in which these scraps of down left the nest. Some claimed that the mother carried them down in her beak; others stoutly maintained that the little ducks climbed down the bole of the nesting tree, using the sharp nails of their webbed feet. In fact, these tiny, nearly-weightless creatures simply tumble out of their nesting tree, fluffy little missiles that do not seem to become injured when they reach the ground and which, for the rest of their time as youngsters, will not again climb into a nesting hole.

Once they have left the nest, very shortly after they are born, for the mother cannot ferry back provisions for them, they follow the duck to the water, leaving it often as they grow older. Eventually they feed with her on insects and vegetable matter, sometimes in the water, at other times exploring the forest floor, the slender voices of the young mingled with the chattering squeals of the adult birds, which, when alarmed, can emit a loud warning cry: whoo...oo-eek!

OUR FIRST DAY in the blind is spent. Dusk has come to the lake, though it is not yet dark. The birds of day call more softly as they settle in the trees; the ducks and the geese quack hoarsely; the nighthawks emit their strange 'peent' cries and make their booms as they pull out of their steep dives. The whip-poor-wills call.

We leave the blind, grateful for the exercise, for we have been cooped up, sitting on our small stools, all this day, unable to stretch properly, breaking the in-between-birds monotony with coffee from the thermos, dining royally on sandwiches that staled quickly in the heat. We are sweat-streaked and weary, and hungry; but we shall return here tomorrow to continue our count. Now, as we board the canoe and push away from the rock island, we begin to think of supper, and of the quiet bush night, and the sound, dreamless sleep that will overtake us quickly once we turn off the gas jets in the cabin and relax on our cots. As we ply through the darkening water, the song of the frogs stills around us but continues to vibrate in the distance.

ANOTHER DAWN is here and the summer is older and we are again concealed inside the blind; we have already made our first entry in our log. A Canada goose came by soon after we settled down to our watch, a big gander, curious about the strange object on the rock island, but evidently unafraid. Perhaps he is the one that charged our canoe in the spring, but he looks peaceful enough now as he swims by, regally, turning his head from side to side, now and then lowering his long neck and dipping his lower mandible in the water while he works his beak with that wet, clacking sound that ducks and geese make when they are feeding. Grey-brown is this bird on his body, darker on the back and at the end of his tail. His sinuous neck is black but for a splash of pure white under the chin that matches the white of his belly and light grey of his chest.

This is Canada's bird, the big honker whose haunting calls in spring and autumn are capable of implanting in man the urges of a strange wanderlust, as though he, too, would take wing and climb the sky and follow the wedge of big Canada's as they speed north or south. This big wild goose is known all over the world; people have admired him for many, many years, have respected him and his kind for their intelligence and courage, and for their fidelity to each other.

Now he raises his head and looks up and the call of another like him is heard. The goose in front of the island answers and soon a second gander comes into view, but in the air this time, and coming fast, already bracing himself for the landing. Keeping his balance with outstretched neck, he uses his fanned tail to ease his momentum, then flaps his wings violently to lessen his speed; in another moment he has dropped almost to water level. Now he touches water. His flat feet and fanned tail brake his speed as they strike against the lake's surface and he sets his wings in the glide position so as to balance his body. Now he is down, amongst a welter of spray and churning water, and he raises his neck and paddles towards his companion. The two 'talk' for a few moments, then they swim away, making for the marsh.

There can hardly be a more thrilling sight than a flock of these big geese coming in to land on the heels of the spring migration; and there can hardly be a bolder, yet more wary, group than these same geese once they have settled on their chosen water. As they come in, before they land, their honking calls turn to a gentle gag-gling which is suddenly increased when the birds sit on water. Now they are weary, but yet they post sentries, two or three birds who have either volunteered for the job or have been 'ordered' to do so by the old ganders who lead the flock. While the others feed, these birds watch for danger and, should they see it, will voice the strident warning call, at the sound of which pandemonium strikes

There are few more thrilling sights than a wedge-shaped flock of Canada geese, with their haunting cries.

Canada geese mate for life. Usually there are five or six eggs, requiring about 30 days of incubation.

the flock. Wings that span six feet thrash water, feet paddle furiously; in an instant the entire flock is airborne and winging away, gaining height with every wing beat.

These birds mate at two years of age and tend to pair for life, mating again only if one of them is killed. Their nests are bulky mounds of sticks and grasses placed on top of a beaver lodge or on a rocky islet, or even on a rock ledge, into the cup of which the goose lays five or six creamy eggs which she incubates for twenty-eight to thirty days. The gander stands guard, ready to die for his mate if need be and capable of breaking a man's arm with one stroke of his powerful wing; and if he needs help, his mate is forever ready to join him. It would take a very bold fox to attack these birds during the breeding season, and even man is wise to give them a wide berth.

Two days after the yellow-green goslings hatch, their father leads them to the water, and the family concentrates on feeding, with both parents guarding the young. More often than not, though now and then, one or the other of the adult birds may wander away on some errand of its own. Now the goslings gain weight rapidly, doubling their size within a week after birth, already beginning to replace some of their down with feathers. But the young geese cannot fly until all their primary feathers are fully grown; and at this time neither can the parents, who, like most ducks and geese, are grounded for almost four weeks during the annual moult.

In the latitude of my lake these birds nest yearly and the ganders that we saw have completed their moult. We have not yet seen the goslings, but by now they, too, will be able to fly, and this is perhaps why the two ganders are here, enjoying their own company, freed for a time of their duty to their mates and their young ones. We hear them again, more distant now, as they enter the marsh. And then we hear them no more.

An hour has passed and the waters we are watching have remained empty. The sun is at high noon, hot as only the summer sun can get, burning into us through the sackcloth so that our bodies trickle with our moisture. But uncomfortable though we are, the heat of the day carries a blessing; it has banished most of the bloodsuckers, and for this we are grateful. Still, it can be monotonous, this watching from a blind at times like these; and uncomfortable, and patience is needed, and I am not an especially patient man. But we wait, silent and hot and cramped; we wait, knowing that sooner or later some bird will come by, perhaps in the air, or walking along the shoreline, or swimming upon the water. To amuse ourselves we try and identify the songs of the birds, and it is then that we see the stealthy green-blue of a crow-sized bird scissoring on long legs on the west bank. 'Green heron,' the entry is made quickly, for this is a scarce bird here, scarce and timid, and I have only seen two others like it.

It walks slowly, with jerky movements, picking its long legs high off the ground, folding them carefully before setting them down again. Its body is blackish-green, glossy; it has a chestnut neck and a white chin and a stripe on its throat, while its green wings are tinged with buff and its underparts are brown-grey and striped, setting off the dull orange of the long legs. As we watch, the bird approaches the water and hops clumsily on to a partly submerged log, one end of which is sticking up in the air. The bird walks up the log and perches, still as a statue on the upthrust end, body and neck held upright, head and long, sharp beak horizontal with the water. For five minutes it remains thus, then, grasping the log with its long toes it pivots headfirst towards the water, using the long beak as a spear. In an instant it bobs up again, using its feet as though they were hinges, and now it has a large bullfrog clamped between its mandibles. Up goes the neck and head and beak; the bird opens its mouth and the struggling frog begins its downward journey to oblivion. For an instant we can see its green back and feet as the bird swallows and we can see, also, how the frog's bulk distends the heron's neck. Thus, we trace the frog's journey to the bird's crop, and we watch as with one last, convulsive swallow the amphibian is disposed of. The bird launches itself from the log and wings slowly towards the north.

Somewhere north of the catkin marsh, this small heron nested and raised its four or five chicks. Both birds took turns guarding the eggs and, later, the young birds, from the predations of the
grackles and crows, one or the other of them remaining always
with the brood in the nest of sticks built perhaps twenty feet from
the ground. Although this bird is not scarce in some areas of the
north country, I have not yet discovered its nesting place near my
lake. And I know not whether there is but one pair here, or two,
or more, for this is difficult country in which to spot a bird that
can 'freeze' at a football that is two hundred yards distant, and
which slips quietly into the bushland when the intruder advances
another hundred steps. The first one that I saw after I had known
this lake for more than one year, I discovered by luck, because a
strong breeze was blowing towards me and the grasses underfoot
had been soaked by a heavy summer rain. Walking silently and into
the wind, I spotted the heron crouched on a leaning poplar sapling
almost at the instant that he saw me. Immediately he was off, but
not before I noted the shaggy head crest which these birds raise
when they are alarmed; and not before he cut loose with his
strange yell of fear, a sound that is hard to set down here, but
which might be described as a staccato, two-syllable 'skee-ow!'

Later, as we drink coffee and eat our stale sandwiches, we see
in quick succession: a beaver swimming towards his lodge, eyeing
the strange new growth on his island, but seeming unconcerned
over its presence; two muskrats, one after the other, swimming
towards the dam; a school of minnows breaking surface, tiny fish,
pockmarking the still water with their blunt little faces; a large
bullfrog emerging from the bottom and swimming to a lily pad,
there to stay for some ten minutes before plopping back into the
water and disappearing amongst the reeds along the west shore; a
constant procession of dragon and damsel flies, seeking mosquitoes; a black squirrel running over the beaver dam, plumed tail
jerking up and down while one of his red relatives, crouched in
the shelter of a cluster of alders, curses him venomously. And again
we listen to the calls of the birds: the redwings and grackles

loudest, for they nest at the northern tip of the marsh and are constantly prospecting their country, now on the catkins, and as quickly scrambling through the bare branches of water-logged poplars and pines; the drumming of woodpeckers, some near, some far; the gurgling song of the marsh wrens; the cheeky voices of the chickadees; the nasal twanging of the nuthatches; the blue jays, loud and harsh, or softly-sweet, as the mood seizes these bush clowns; the crows, croaking calls coming from all directions at once; the laughter of the flickers, high shrill, hysterical.

Still the lake around us is empty of birds and at last we must move. This day is just too hot, there is little moving on the water. The sun is still high as we leave our steaming blind and scramble gratefully into the canoe, paddling to our landing place in but five minutes. Now we are beset by mosquitoes as we disturb their shelters, the undersides of the alder leaves, the stems of the grasses. Small clouds fly up and seek our bodies and we hastily spray ourselves with the repellent, but some get through and we shall itch later. We beach the canoe quickly, for we must leave the edge of the lake or collect many more bites. As we climb a slope and break out of the ring of shrubs that marks the lake on nearly all of its boundaries, we see the lazy, circling shape of a turkey vulture, the black, scavenging ghost of the skies. As we pause and watch the big bird, he appears to become interested in our movements, for he circles overhead and comes a little lower, so that we can see his spread 'fingers,' and the lean red head that moves constantly from side to side.

He is all beautiful motion, that ugly carrion eater. On the ground, or seen close-to, he is repulsive; he smells; he carries the look of death upon his wings. His beak is hideous, his gaping nostrils are unclean slits in the ivory-tipped beak; his pasty-white eye patches forming wrinkled half-circles under his eyes are like the puffy bags left by debauch upon some evil, ageing lecher. But look at him now as he soars so effortlessly up there against the blue! Can any flying thing perform with such grace those intricate, fluid glides and spirals? The six-foot wings are held immobile but for the quivering of the wind through those black fingers at their ends. Now he hangs motionless upon an updraught, then he spirals again, performing his ballet for our benefit. Upwards he soars, higher and higher into the empty sky until, at last, he is but a black speck that finally becomes too small for our eyes to follow.

Somewhere to the north are the nesting grounds of these birds, not numerous here, to be sure, but still in sufficient numbers to effectively clean the forest of carrion. Each pair has chosen some rock cave, or hollow stump, or thicket in which to lay two brownish eggs upon whatever nature has put upon the forest floor, be it bare rock, or rotting wood, or dead leaves and twigs. There the downy-white young will hatch, harpy-like chicks come to life upon a nesting surface that is yet clean, but that will soon be soiled by the rotting juices of carrion disgustingly regurgitated by the parent birds. Two days after birth the nest would be easily located by its stench, if we were to find ourselves fifteen or twenty feet from it, but these strange hatchlings of the wild thrive on their diet of putrid, half-digested meat which is thrust, warm and slimy, down their gulping throats. About two months after hatching, the gangling black youngsters try their wings, jogging off clumsily with laboured flaps until they are beating air. Then, as though by magic, the ugly chicks become transformed into lithe and graceful flying things, masters of clean air bent on a scavenging mission.

We turn to go, heading south along the ragged and ageing logging road that leads to the asphalt highway, for this offers better walking in the heat, and there will be fewer flies on it. At our feet grows the green grass that is laced with the curled dead leaves of last year, around us the songs of the birds; pressing down on us the heat that is drawing the moisture out of our bodies. To some people we must seem mad, forsaking the cool comforts of civilized living; but we are not demented; uncomfortable, yes; but exhilarated. And we feel the fullness of life that surrounds us and that is a part of us; we feel it pulsing in our bodies as our vital juices course through their channels, feeding tissue and muscle and sinew and bone, rallying tired parts, nourishing constantly;

while deep within us the chemical factories of life work constantly to supply the complex demands of our blood.

We walk slowly, for to move quickly is too great an effort, and we flush the resting grouse and her brood of fledged chicks. The hen whistles her sharp warning as she scuttles towards us, pretending that she had broken wing while her chicks buzz through the air like small brown rockets, flying four or five feet above the forest floor, short flights that are resumed as quickly as they end. We count ten chicks as they crash past us and lose themselves in the bush and we watch as the hen makes her fast recovery and rises from the ground to join her young. We hear their agitated progress through the thick bush and we hear the hen's continuing, peeping whistle. Then we hear them no more, and we know that she has led them to some quiet spot, perhaps two hundred feet away, and that now the chicks will be crouching immobile, while the hen struts stealthily, a quiet, alert sentry who will not relax until the last of our footsteps become silenced.

We have reached the halfway section of the old road. We pause for a rest beside a gnarled young oak that exhibits upon its trunk, on the west face of it, a healed blaze mark. I put that there four years ago, a boundary marker necessary then, for I was still exploring this country. The tree has grown new tissue over the old wound, which has closed inwardly, showing still a fine line in its centre, the edges of the scar and protuberance. And the foot of the oak is a large, orange mushroom, an *amanita muscaria*, deadly fly amanita; a species which has become abundant in this wilderness. A beautiful killer for man and some of the creatures of the wilderness, succulent feed for others, a mushroom almost one foot in circumference which has still some of the white splotches of its birth cowl adhering to its upper surface; a fungus that is still wearing the demure little skirt that was formed when the umbrella head thrust free of the forest mulch. We look at it; I photograph it, placing upon its centre a twenty-five cent coin, so that it will indicate the size of this monster mushroom when the picture is printed.

A little farther away now. Again we flush a bird, another grouse, a lone cock that rattles off into the forest, the drumming of his stubby wings startling loud. Perhaps he mated the hen we saw just now; perhaps not, for there are many grouse here. Now he, too, is gone and is silent, waiting for us to pass so that he can squat again in the shade of the tree or rock, there to take his ease until the coolness of evening and the urge of his belly drive him to search for plant buds and insects.

Six or seven weeks ago this bird and others like him were busy with their mating dances, with their challenges and love songs, with their fights and with the mating of their hens. Strutting royally upon some downed log, the cock grouse postures vainly. He stands very erect and lifts his crest and the soft, dark-blue collar of feathers around his neck, forming the ruff that has given him his name. He stands still, begins to beat the air with his wings; slowly at first, then gathering momentum, faster, faster...and now his wings are a blur. Thus, he beats out his famous repertoire, at once a challenge to other males that he has claimed this territory as his, and a love call to the hens in the area; bup...bup...bup-bup-bup-errr. Again and again he repeats his drum-call, then perhaps he will move to another log, for he will have several in his territory which he will use for this purpose, by day or night, during the full of the breeding season.

Eventually a hen will come to him and will wait for a time, crouched under a deadfall tree, or in the shelter of balsam or pine and, when she arrives, the cock will stop his drumming and strut towards her making a loud hissing noise. The hen has been won; she is ready to be bred, but the capricious cock mistakes her for a rival (or does he merely show off his superior powers?). At any rate, he pecks at her, dragging both his wings, now and then jumping, striking at her with his claws; and the hen retreats from his royal presence, but not too far away! She waits nearby, knowing that in a day or two her lord will notice her, and she will be mated.

When the mating is over, the cocks go their solitary ways while the hens busy themselves with nest building. A simple process, but one which evidently requires great care in the selection of the right building site. This place, which must offer concealment and shelter from the frosts of April and May, is usually a depression in the land that is guarded by fallen tree branches, or perhaps it could be a suitable place under some downed tree stump. There she lays from ten to fifteen buff-coloured eggs, rather like those of the domestic hen, which she incubates for twenty-eight days, sitting immobile, a mottled brown bump on the forest floor, invisible to all but the keenest, most patient observer.

When the chicks hatch they face the world soaking wet, their yellowish-brown-streaked bodies shivering bundles of fluff. But in a surprisingly short time the little chicks dry off, and are immediately ready to follow mother through the wilderness, peeping shrilly if they lose sight of her, 'freezing' invisibly if they believe danger is present. At this time, hawks are perhaps their most persistent enemies, but their greatest danger is the weather, for these little birds, so tough and strong once they grow their feathers, chill very easily, and perhaps half the brood will die before June gives way to July. But those that survive into that month do well on a diet of wild berries and plant buds and insects, and before the end of summer each goes his own way.

When winter comes the grouse change their footwear. In summer and autumn their feet are chicken-like; in winter they grow comb-like projections on both sides of their toes which act as snowshoes, allowing them to walk upon even the lightest snow crust. Sometimes, when the snow is new and a cold night is in the offing, they punch holes in drifts and shelter there. And on occasion, after a night of cold that plunges the thermometer down to twenty and thirty degrees below zero, they have a hard struggle to break out of their snow chambers.

At times, a person may walk almost on top of these birds before they explode in fast, violent flight, always taking care to put the girth of trees between themselves and their most persistent

enemy. At other times, they will move away silently long before someone gets near them, but at all times they are aware of intruders. Today, we have been lucky to see more than one bird. But for now, we have recorded them in our log, one more species that lives in the area of my lake. And now, at last, we go home, to the cabin, to rest within its coolness.

ELEVEN

AUGUST IS HERE; the time of young animals and fledgling birds, and of ripe berries for the picking, and of blue skies and long days of sun; and of dryness so dangerous that one careless spark can convert this forest country into a raging furnace. August, and unbidden memories of last year's autumnal migration are followed by thoughts of the first snows and of the arrival of winter. August, when the blackflies have passed and the mosquitoes are waning and some of the leaves are already beginning to turn. August, the harvest time, when the bear packs lard under his hide and the deer fawns are losing their spots and the bucks wear their antlers proudly, adornments which are now almost completely formed and are sheathed in soft 'velvet' that has not yet begun to tatter.

We have now abandoned our blind, for we have finished with most of the waterbirds and we are now looking for the songsters, the warblers and the grosbeaks and the catbirds and pheobes and vireos and many others. Now our task is pleasant. No longer do we have to sweat it out under the canvas shelter, sitting for cramped hours and eating stale foods. Instead, we roam through the area, walking softly, always alert for some new bird, field glasses ready.

On this day we have crossed the lake, walking along the lip of the beaver dam, and we are watching a sturdy bird with a bright rose V-patch on his breast. A little smaller than a robin (that is, a North American robin, for the European species of 'redbreast' are but the size of a chickadee), the rose-breasted grosbeak male is now free of parental responsibility and he sings his praises to the skies. His voice is melodious, clear, a sustained song not unlike that of the robin. He sits perched on a young poplar tree, his heavy, pinkish beak opening and closing with his song, his black head and back and wings shining in the sunlight, accentuating the whiteness of the lower part of his body and of the irregular patches that break

up the solid ebony of his back. He is gripping his perch with feet that are pale blue and which match the shade of his sturdy legs.

Yesterday we saw a female of this species. Now we are struck by the contrast between the two. The gorgeous male bears no resemblance to his mate, except for size and the general appearance of beak and shape. She is no less beautiful, but subdued in her shades, going in for browns that are streaked with off-white and delicately pastelled yellow on the breast. Each year the males and females of the species fly north from South America and Central Mexico to breed in eastern United States and in southern Canada.

Often as not, the male helps his mate build her nest of small twigs and grasses that is anchored in the crook of some branch ten feet or so above ground, a nest that seems almost unsuitable as a nursery, for it is so loosely built that it can be seen through when looked at from the bottom. In this seemingly flimsy saucer the female lays three, four, or five brown-spotted, pale blue eggs and she and her mate take turns sitting on them. Which is unusual, for, as a rule, male birds that are brightly coloured seldom help in this task, sensibly keeping away from the eggs lest their brightness attract an enemy. But not the grosbeak male! He seems to disdain the perils of his colourful dress and blandly sits on the nest, adding a touch of bravado to the act by singing his tuneful melody while he warms his unborn young, a sort of whistle-while-you-work approach!

Now the grosbeak has gone. We walk again, but we are quickly arrested by a plaintive mewing coming from a tangled thicket of poplars and alders near the marsh. Can it be that a kitten is lost out here? No. This is the voice of a catbird, so named because of its plaintive call; a bird between eight and nine inches long, of sleek proportions and longish tail. It is slate grey almost all over, but a black stripe along the crown of its head and a deep rusty patch under its tail feathers break the monotonous sobriety of its main garment. We stop and squat, keeping still, searching the tangle of green with our eyes as our ears listen to the mewing which is now and again interrupted by a medley of scrambled notes, none of which are repeated once they have been uttered.

Now we see it. It is perched on a stub in a dead poplar, its brownish legs gripping tightly the smooth branch, its body in a crouch, so that the fairly-broad tail points upwards, above the extended head with the slim, sharp beak. Its wings are dragging by its sides, a characteristic pose of this shy bird of the dense woods.

Often this bird mimics the songs of other forest birds, but each note is uttered once, a fact which tends to give him away to his human listeners, for most song birds repeat the same notes over and over again. Now, because he knows we are here, he is mewing and his tail points upwards and he holds the quick-get-away crouch. But when he is unaware of observers, he frequently holds his tail downwards and he holds his body close to the branch upon which he is perched. At times, becoming suddenly bold, he flies to the top of a bush or small tree and can be plainly seen. Occasionally, during late spring and early summer, he may be seen in the open, searching out insects, which seem to be his favourite food.

Winging northward at night from his breeding grounds in Panama, the catbird male arrives in the area where he intends to look for a mate; his first job, once he has regained the vigour he lost during his long flight, is to stake out his home territory and tell his rivals in the area that he will fight for his choice. This he does in a series of mews, mixed with warblings and seemingly-impromptu notes of threat. Then, when the females arrive, he wastes no time in wooing the one of his choice.

The courtship is fast and furious. Sighting his chosen mate, the male begins a mad dashing through the underbrush. It looks aimless, but a close observer will quickly see that he is always in hot pursuit of his lady, interrupting his dashing when he has captured her attention, to strut about on a branch, wings down by his sides, tail up, while he now and then stops still and bursts into song. But the wooing is short; two or three days later the pair settle down to domesticity. Now 'Mr. Catbird' tells the world of his conquest. He sings repeatedly through the day and goes so far as to carry his concert into the night. It was not until quite recently that I identified

the mysterious songster that often stopped me during some of my walks through the darkened forest. I was frankly fooled, not registering the catbird's abilities to mock, trying to pick out the notes so that I could classify the night songster; until common sense came to my rescue and a lucky flash of my light beam picked up his silhouette atop a young poplar near my cabin.

While 'Mister' now enjoys himself, 'Mrs. Catbird' is busy nest-building, first choosing a site low to the ground located within dense cover. Here she uses sticks and bark and leaves and grass to fashion the nest, which she lines with plant rootlets and soft, inner shreds of dead tree bark. In this nest she lays between three and five green-blue eggs and incubates them for about thirteen days, following which the baby 'cats' come into the world, red and naked and wobbly, with big heads and bulbous closed eyes, and soft beaks that are forever opening to receive food.

Now, both parent birds are kept busy hunting the insects upon which their young subsist almost entirely, and if the father now and then breaks away to feast on wild fruits, who can blame him? But if he plays truant now and then, he is quick to respond to his mate's cry of distress. In fact, catbirds own a quality which few other birds or mammals possess; they will often rush to the rescue of babies other than their own and are always ready to adopt a brood of young catbirds orphaned by predators.

We leave the catbird in the concealment of his green realm, but we have walked for only five minutes when we are arrested by a repeated, clear call: Towee...towee...towee. The bird is perhaps one inch smaller than the catbird, but whereas the slate-coloured mewer is shy, the towhee is pert and unafraid. He is busy ground-scratching under a spruce, his light-coloured legs moving quickly, his actions similar, but more constant, than those of a hen scratching for feed. His sharp, heavy beak is black; his eyes are ruby with dark pupils. On his chest and back and wings he is mostly black, though a few flashes of white are seen on his wings and back as he moves. His sides are what immediately attract us; they are a beautiful, rusty-cinnamon colour that gradually gives way to

white on his lower chest and belly and ends, bisected by the black, amongst the fluffy feathers that cloak his tail root. Again he sings his two-syllable call, hardly bothering to pause in his busy scratching, the while dipping down quickly with his strong beak to pick up worm or insect.

Soon he is joined by his mate, more subdued, but no less beautiful. Where he is black, she is light cinnamon. And if her rufus side patches are not as bright as her spouse's, still, they contrast with the pastels of her head and chest and back and tail, the rounded end of which is rimmed, like her mate's, with white bars that are longest on the outside of the tail. Gradually, they shorten as they advance towards its centre, never quite covering the entire end of the tail. Like him also, her lower chest and belly are white, and she has his sturdy beak and ruby eyes.

Each is busy now, scratching for insects with which to feed their brood of six, born in a loosely-built nest of bark and leaves and twigs which she later lined with fine grasses and lanks of any animal hair or fur that she could find. In this nest she sat, her cinnamon-brown back making her almost invisible for the twelve days during which she incubated the white eggs which were dotted with small brown flecks.

As we watch, a purple finch male arrives, landing several feet away from the towhees. We note the species in our log and we must wonder at this bird's name, for his colourful body is dressed not in purple, but in a palish raspberry colour. Deepest at the top-knot on his head, the colour tone creeps down his breast to fade into white on his lower chest and stomach, holds its bright hue amongst dark stripes on his back, emerges pure again as it nears the tail, and fades into buffy-brown amongst the tail feathers. The wings of this bird are barred dark brown or black and laced with white that has a faint suspicion of his raspberry hue. Purple finch indeed!

Above our heads his mate lands on a pine bough. She looks like him in outline; she has the same sparrow-like beak and the stripes on the back and wings, but her overall colour is light-

brown and her chest is heavily barred, showing little of the off-white with which the bars are laced. Now the male sings, a light warble, tuneful and airy, impossible to describe on paper, which he ends with a clear tink, sounding rather like some hard object scraping lightly over a metal pot.

This pair nested in a pine almost forty feet from the ground, for I discovered their home site when they were building it. In the completed cup, made of grasses and roots and lined with anything soft the birds could find, four light-blue eggs, brown-spotted at their large ends, were laid, and during the time that she sat on them, the male entertained her with his charming arias while he hunted and brought her food. The brood is born and both birds are on the prowl. Both have now found something for their young and they fly off, leaving the busy towhees scratching in almost the identical spots at which they landed. It is time for us to move too.

SUMMER IS A TIME for leisure for such as me. I distract quickly from my purpose, I idle, but though I appear lazy at such times, I do not just sit aimlessly in my wilderness. There are times, though, such as now, when I become tired of a steady pursuit; and perhaps you will, by this time, share my feelings, so we shall play truant for a while. We shall leave the birds to their tasks, listening to their voices often and seeing quick glimpses of them now and then. But I, for one, am off on a trip of aimless exploration that will reward me, I know, with a host of new experiences, with more knowledge of the wilderness, with a richer life. Usually I like to take these trips alone, for I find that the company of my kind distracts me, and seldom do I encounter a soul kindred enough to remain silent when I do not want to talk and to stop to listen to the forest when I want to listen. On occasion, Joan comes with me for part of the distance, then she turns back, for I am apt to go anywhere and do almost anything at these times. And although she is the only other being in this wilderness with whom I can be at ease and still enjoy the life that teems around us, she has had some uncomfortable experiences when she has followed me deep into the summer bush. So now, she comes along the routes she knows will not be quite so wild, then she returns to our cabin while I roam where the fancy takes me, stop when I want, look at what I want, listen to the wilderness, smell it, talk to it in silent voice, feel it. So that, normally, if you came to visit my wilderness, I would not invite you out with me at a time like this, but now it is different; through these pages you, too, can walk, for you will have to remain silent and stop at the right times and be patient, else you will turn back and I will go one alone.

IT IS A PERFECT MORNING in midsummer; early. The sun is above the trees, the sky is clean and blue. It will be hot this day, already I know this, though it is all coolness and freshness outside now and the scent of summer is a blessing granted to a man fortunate enough to be in a place like this at a time like this. The pines waft their gummy, heady scent upon the air, the grass smell is clear, the strong odour of the poplars is a pleasant spice. Last night a skunk passed near the cabin. It did not discharge its smell, but the scent of the creature clings faintly to the ground.

A meadow vole—unlikely to be seen except by the most observant.

This day the wind is quiet. Its absence and the peace of this forest, and the gladness in the voices of its birds, and the scurrying of the squirrels, and its trees and plants and shrubs and wild flowers and grasses remind me of William Wordsworth. I stop to think about Wordsworth, and I remember the city that I have escaped from, and the lines of the poet run through my mind.

> The world is too much with us; late and soon,
> Getting and spending we lay waste our powers;
> Little we see in nature that is ours;
> We have given our hearts away, a sordid boon!
> This Sea that bears her bosom to the moon;
> The winds that will be howling at all hours,
> And are up-gathered now like sleeping flowers;
> For this, for everything, we are out of tune;
> It moves us not. Great God! I'd rather be
> A pagan suckled in a creed outworn;
> So might I, standing on this pleasant lea,
> Have glimpses that would make me less forlorn;
> Have sight of Proteus rising from the sea;
> Or hear old Triton blow his wreathed horn.

Powerful lines these, written by a man dead a century and more ago, yet as valid now as they were when he penned them. Once I did not see the beauty in this verse. Today, I am moved by the sea and the moon and the winds. Today, I stand upon a pleasant lea and if I do not have sight of Proteus or hear Triton's horn, still I have sight of the wonders of creation and sound of the creatures of Diana as they travel through this living land that so many men can neither understand nor appreciate. And I have not given my heart away getting and spending in the city. And I see much in nature that is mine and I have it in me to marvel at the understanding of Wordsworth. Indeed, upon such a day as this I feel I must be sharing the visions which prompted him to write his verse. Am I a

pagan then? Perhaps. Or maybe I am a Christian, for Wordsworth's lines bring to mind another writing, contained in the Bible, in the Book of Job.

> But ask now the beasts, and they shall teach thee; and the
> fowls of the air, and they shall tell thee:
> Or speak to the earth, and it shall teach thee; and the
> fishes of the seas shall declare unto thee.

No, I am not a pagan. Neither am I a Christian in the fullness of the word, for I practise no organized religion and most of my beliefs would shock the dogmatic ones. But I believe in this creation that surrounds me, and I learn from it, and I speak to it; and whether it hears me or not, matters not, for I hear myself say that which the wilderness has placed within me. And on mornings like this there is much to learn and much to say within the silent reaches of the mind. So enough of this, let us go out into the wilderness. It has already placed its mark upon me, and, this I promise you: if you follow me this day, it will place its mark upon you also.

ONE HOUR HAS PASSED and the heat of late August has us in its grip. Black streaks of sweat stain our shirts, drops of moisture trickle down our breastbones to soak into the waistbands of our trousers. The brow drips, the palms sweat, the scalp prickles. But to me this is not unpleasant. It is merely a very small price that the wilderness exacts in payment of the things that it will show us this day. We sit now under a shaggy balsam, grateful for its shade. We sit unmoving, silent, our eyes and our ears and our noses busy, seeking moving life in this now seemingly-empty forest. Five minutes pass and lengthen into ten and still we are unmoving. We must wait.

Ahead of us stands a clump of hemlocks, tall evergreens of feathery needles and broad of beam. Something is disturbing the branches of one of them. We watch. A brown, indistinct body lurches into view, then another. Grouse, those ruffed wild chickens of the forest. They are young, these birds, spring chicks already

Ruffed grouse, the wild chickens of the forest.

almost full grown. They sit in the hemlock, sated from picking the wild strawberries and blueberries; they sit with feathers puffed out as insulation against the heat; they sit with beaks open, thus cooling the interior of their bodies.

They heard us coming and they concealed themselves from us, but now they have forgotten us and they have become accustomed to our still shapes. One closes its beak for an instant and then opens it again in a giant yawn; its eyes become heavy-lidded, turn into slits, close altogether and the bird's head nods. It opens its eyes again and shuffles more comfortably on its roost. The other bird stretches, standing upright on the branch and flapping its wings three times, almost unseating its companion, then both of them settle to peaceful rest. Now it is time for us to move on, for I have decided to go to the second beaver lake and the journey is long.

We rise. The grouse become instantly alert, but they do not fly away. Instead they watch our quiet passage through their territory, twisting their necks as we pass behind them. Finally they lose us as the forest swallows our backs, but they will remain alert until the noise of our passing has died.

Underfoot the wild grass is long, concealing many things and offering itself as fodder to a host of others. Again I stop, for an old notion has come to me; we are walking upon the very seeds of life and our great, flat feet encased in their heavy leather coverings are crushing and killing with each step we take. But we're made as we are and this killing is unavoidable, still we move with a little more care and we try to avoid the more obvious bits of life that crowd our path. And, in this manner, we see the aphids clustered about one stem of a wild bramble plant.

How many are there tightly-packed upon the four-inch shoot? They would be almost impossible to count. Thousands, certainly. We pause over the plant and the insects, then see a column of little red ants scurrying up and down the stalk. Closer we bend, and my magnifier comes out, and we study the aphids and the little red ants.

The tiny insects are feeding on the plant sap; they are glutting themselves as they eat, as their body converts that which they cannot use into plant sugars. Now and then one of the insects defecates; but this is not excreta that is produced from the minute anus, it is a globule of crystal-clear sugar. And this is what the ants are here for. Now we can see that those ants advancing up the stalk towards the aphids are normal in size, while those that are crawling over the insects and those that are hurrying down the stalk have distended abdomens. We watch more closely. We see an aphid excrete its honey dew and we see an ant grasp the fat little insect with its front legs, while it sucks greedily of the newly-released plant sugars. This ant has already sucked honey dew from other aphids, now it is full, its red belly distended to seemingly-dangerous proportions. It leaves the aphids and hurries away to its nest, there to feed the colony's larvae with this strangely-manufactured nectar. We see more crystal globules come from more aphids and then we note that when an ant has failed to find an already-discharged supply of nectar, it strokes a likely-looking aphid with its thin front legs. And sometimes it is rewarded by a new globule of honey dew, seemingly released by the insect after the ant's legs stimulated its body into excretion. But at times an ant must massage several aphids

before it is rewarded, for the nectar takes a little time to be manufactured by the digestive system of an insect and, once it has emptied its bowels, it cannot fill them again at will.

We watch, for there is fascination here. Endlessly the ants file back and forth, 'milking' food from the bowels of the aphids. Endlessly the insects press together, each competing with its neighbour for a bit of stem to suck, so that the tender shoot would seem to be coated by tiny, shiny, rounded grains of blue-black sand. Why are they so close-packed at this place when there are more tender green shoots for the sucking upon this very plant? We know not this answer, but I would guess at it. Perhaps the stickiness of the sugary nectar that they discharge makes its removal necessary, else its water content might soon evaporate and the aphids become trapped in a glue of their manufacture. Perhaps by clustering together in one place they make the job of their nurses, the ants, easier?

Looking still more closely at the insects we see slight differences amongst them. Some have wings, and these are the migrating females who will soon leave to begin a colony of their own. Others are so tiny that even with the powerful pocket glass they are nearly invisible, these are the young. Around the stem upon which the colony is feeding, there are the plant's leaves. On some of these leaves small galls have been formed, shiny, smooth little swellings that house a smaller colony of aphids, protecting them from attack, isolating them from their nurse ants. And we wonder what is happening inside one of these, and particularly we wonder what is happening to the honey dew that the insects must discharge. So we take one of these galls and we slice it open with a penknife and inside it we see a mixture of things. There are large aphids and small ones, and smaller ones yet; and we see tiny, oval-black, glistening eggs, and we see a sort of green dust. But we do not see the drops of honey dew. Do the small-small aphids feed on this? Does the honey dew, somehow, become converted into the greenish dust that we see? We make a mental note to question the first friendly entomologist that we meet, for we do not have the answers we seek.

Now we are moving through dense, mixed timber. Here there are evergreens and hardwoods, alders and hazels and willows, all melting into a thick screen of shade that draws to itself many forms of life. The going is hard, but our pace is leisurely, for speed matters not here, and is, in fact, our enemy; only leisure gives our eyes time to see, and our ears time to hear, and our noses time to smell. We pause often; sometimes we just stand, listening and looking and smelling; at other times we sit upon some dead log and we let the forest envelop us so that it even manages to invade our minds. And we feel, if only for a short time, the true, primeval freedom that every living thing of the wilderness enjoys.

After one of these stops we must scramble over a toppled giant tree. It is a poplar and it died many years ago, but some of its branches still hold their shape and point starkly towards the sky. As we clear this obstacle, we see an immobile shape sheltered by long grasses and ferns and we must stop and examine it. We see before us a snowshoe hare leveret, which is perhaps five or six days old. It sits so still one might pass it without seeing it. Of course it knows we are here, and thus it seeks refuge in stillness and camouflage, for it has not yet attained the great speed of its mother; but as we make no threatening move towards it, as we remain immobile, it slowly abandons its caution. First it sits on its back haunches, its fuzzy little ears sweeping the area for sound of enemies, then it yawns and lifts small front paws to its muzzle and begins to 'wash' its face and head and ears. Now it has finished and it bends to nibble at green shoots, ignoring our presence. Slowly it wanders away, taking little hops, stopping often to feed.

On again. And now the terrain has changed. The dense thicket is gone and instead we tread on granite that must be a million years old. Mosses grow here, and small plants, and a few stunted trees. Lizards seek coolness and insects under flat rocks, ants scurry in search of food, spiders build their webs between rock cracks or upon small plants. Birds are here feeding, warblers and flickers and blackbirds and wrens. We see them and we hear their song as the noon sun presses hard upon us, and the blue sky pales in

contrast to this molten fire that has reached us after travelling through an immensity of space.

A game trail leads along the eastern skirts of the beaver lake over terrain that quickly becomes clogged with blueberry bushes. The purple-blue berries are inviting and we stop to pick some, eating as we pick and communing with bees and a host of other insects; some come to drink nectar from the white, cup-like flowers that the plants still bear, others feed on the shiny green leaves, still others are eating of the sweet berries. We eat perhaps one good handful apiece, refreshed by these provisions of the wilderness, yet slightly cloyed by the sweetness of them. It would be nice to dispel this aftertaste of our gluttony, for under this sun our mouths will soon become thickened, furry. We wish for something clean and sharp with which to refresh our palates. And nature provides. Snuggling under the shade of some sparse hazels, there is a cluster of wintergreen and we pick three or four of the dark-green leaves and stuff them into our mouths. We chew them and soon the sweetness of the berries is gone and we are cleansed by the aromatic juices of this medicinal plant. We stroll onwards, chewing thoughtfully.

We have walked for perhaps four miles. We have passed my lake, climbed a slight rock rise and have crossed the second lake by walking over the lip of the dam. Now we stand at the far northern end of this larger body of water. We are hemmed in by forest. Before us the lake stretches south for perhaps one mile, its surface covered by lilies, by their blooms and their leaves. Now we feel the fullness of the wilderness, for there are no other humans within miles of us, there is no roar of traffic, no babble of raised voices, no sign of human habitation. We are here, fully alone, enmeshed within the living green of a great forest place and here, for us, there is utter peace.

The wilderness, at times like this, massages the mind. It becomes a tranquilizer, eradicating the irritating concerns of modern city humdrum; it removes the tension from muscles held too taut for their efficient functioning. The mind is loosened up; the

body is relaxed. We sit, silent, of course, and we look and listen and allow the wilderness to nudge our minds in whatever direction it pleases.

A black duck comes sedately from out of a patch of rushes, moving with the purposeful grace of a sailing clipper running before a fair wind. A muskrat surfaces and climbs laboriously upon one of its feeding rafts, dropping from its mouth the little bundle of catkin stems which it has brought here to eat. It rises on its haunches and inspects its environment, seeking danger. It can find none and it settles to its feast, now and then pausing to inspect one of the many bank swallows that flit tirelessly back and forth over the lake, hunting insects. The rat feeds, the ducks swim, the swallows gape flies, the birds sing, the forest murmurs; we sit in silence, entranced by the wilderness, embraced by it, human animals returned to their original setting. Can you not, if you search deep within your innermost being, see the mark which this walk through my wilderness has placed upon you this day? If you cannot, I pity you, for we must retrace our steps, we must go back to our birds and you many never have another chance to find your soul in the depth of this greenness.

AUGUST IS TIRING. Already its sun has lost some of its fire and the leaves of the deciduous trees are beginning to brown and curl. This year's nestling birds are fully-fledged and hunting on their own and their parents are bedecked in their new feathers. Bird voices fill the air, flocks of congregating fliers can be seen in meadow and tree, a procession of songsters not yet ready to take the skyways south, but made restless by the waning sun of late August.

The animals of the wilderness are showing the fat of good summer living; those that will stay active and face the soon-to-be storms of autumn and winter are resplendent in their new, thick coats; those that will soon seek shelter in underground den or hollow tree are sleek with the fat of good eating that must see them through until next spring again brings strong sunlight.

In the backwoods the bears are glossy-fat, their coats shining

and almost prime. The timber wolf pups are sizeable and hunting for themselves while the adults take their ease after a hard summer spent training their offspring. The foxes glow chestnut and ebony in the early light of morning, their black stockings shiny, sooty columns that move with accustomed stealth through the under-brush. The beaver is busy already with his poplar trees, chipping and tearing with his great teeth, felling and cutting and carrying and embedding tender branches in the mud of lake bottom, his rations for winter.

This is another in-between time in the wilderness. Summer has not quite gone, the freshness of autumn can be felt in the air and evenings carry a new bite to them. September is yet to come and October is unused. Perhaps a spell of Indian Summer will bring back memories of the few candid months that we have spent wandering through this labyrinthine forest in search of our birds. But after that, surely, will come true autumn with its winds and its frosts and its powers to kill the leaves, to strip them from their boughs so that they will return to the earth, there to be coated with wet and with snow; there to be worked on by the invisible scavengers of the wilderness, who will soften them and prepare their dead bodies for the new growing season next year. And while these things are taking place, the birds will begin to fly south, the geese and the ducks, and the herons and the bitterns; the owls and the hawks and the vultures; the warblers and robins and catbirds, and grackles and orioles, and many others. And if you are still with me then you will stand with me, beside my lake and you will stare at the sky as the birds of day pass overhead; the geese up there high, arrowing their way to the warm lands, calling their sad songs of farewell; the ducks whistling lower, their hoarse voices also bidding us goodbye for another year.

We have counted eighty-six different species of birds during this interlude of warmth. And yet there are more here, some of which we have heard but not seen, others which I know live here but which have remained hidden from our eyes. It matters not now that we should list them all here, for any one of us can quickly find such

lists already printed if we wish to read an alphabetical table of bird species. But we have seen more than birds; we have heard more than their voices. We have entered this wilderness and come to terms with it and we carry in our minds pictures of its moods and its ways which will remain forever a part of our beings. We have seen the forces of nature exerted pitilessly upon the land and all that it contains; we have smelled the wetness of the forest after a rain; we have sniffed the aroma of drought; we have been an intimate part of all these things and we have learned a few of the secrets of creation.

Yet, there is much to learn still and, as you leave me, I am already planning future journeys through this wilderness. I want to press deeper into it and walk trails that are strange to me and seek more of those mysteries that Creation so grudgingly reveals to the inquisitive ones who dare to pursue them into the very heart of her creation. It now remains to close the last chapter of this narrative, to take you with me in word one more time, through another autumn and perhaps into the beginning of another winter. And if we are lucky, we may yet solve a few more puzzles here.

TWELVE

IF THERE BE a finer time in the wilderness than late September I know it not. The flame of the maples glows already, the yellows of the poplars are beginning to come; the evergreens look fresh against the vividness of early autumnal colours. The timber wolf howls at night, the hare startles quickly, the winds come more often and blow more coldly and the pulse of man must beat a little faster at the prospects of another savage winter that is just lingering a short distance away.

The first time that I saw my lake, September had gone and October was ageing, and I missed this interlude of softness. But a year later I stood upon the beaver lodge on the rock island in the lake and I watched the sun climb down the western treeline. And I listened to the forest murmur and I heard the wind strumming through the outstretched pinions of the wild goose. I wondered then about the migration of birds and I determined to seek answers to the many questions that framed themselves in my mind. Now I have some of these answers and it is fitting that I should set them down here, on the eve of another autumn, for soon the birds will take wing again.

Once, more or less recently, it occurred to me to wonder why we do not see vast numbers of birds fly southward in the autumn. True, ducks and geese and some of the larger birds are a common sight in spring and fall, but the thousands upon thousands of small birds that live in Canada in summer do not fill our daylight skies. Pondering over this, I decided that if these songsters could not be seen migrating north or south, it followed that they travelled at night. Thus, I searched the literature for confirmation of my idea to discover that I was right, for many of our smaller birds do, indeed, travel at night and can be seen silhouetted against a full moon if one uses powerful glasses and has the patience to keep

them trained on the moon's surface. Possessed of this information, the next question was quick to follow: Why do some birds migrate at night and others migrate during the day?

Answers to these queries are more complex and still not entirely certain. It has, though, been reasonably established that those birds that travel at night have within themselves navigational aids that allow them to orient themselves by the stars, while those that travel during the day use the sun as a guide or merely follow a route that has been taught them by their parents during their first autumnal migration south and their first spring migration north.

To attempt to set down in a few short pages of a book all the events that led to the discovery of some of the mysteries of bird migration is an impossible task. At best I can only hope to provide a few facts, for there is much that we do not yet know, and while it has been more or less established that some birds are oriented by the stars and others by the sun, we do not know how their hidden 'compasses' operate, or even where they are located within the bodies of the birds. And, what is perhaps more important, we do not know with any degree of certainty what stimulates the birds to migration at just the right times. We do not even know why some birds migrate and others do not, and though we can today guess that the availability of food and over-crowding in temperate regions probably lies behind the habit of migration, we do not know how this habit became established. We are reduced to guessing that the ice ages, by reducing ancient forests to frozen, food-less wastes, drove the birds south and that, unaccountably, after the ice retreated and the northern forests grew again, the birds of the day retained an inherited memory of their ancestral breeding grounds and began to return to them in the spring.

How do birds know when it is time to migrate in spring and autumn? Each spring some 200 different species of birds flock to northern US and Canada to breed and 'summer;' as inevitably, they turn southward in the autumn to winter in southern US and in Central and South America. It might be supposed that fluctuations

in temperature drive the birds on their migrations, but because birds usually arrive at their winter or spring grounds at approximately the same time each season, regardless of freak weather conditions, this supposition would be wide of the mark. But scientific laboratory tests tend to show that the shortening days of autumn and the lengthening days of late winter and spring trigger certain endocrine glands within the brain and bodies of the birds into releasing stimulating hormones. And what, you might well ask, is an endocrine gland? It is part of one of the body's two main control systems. The first of these is the nervous system; the second the endocrine system, which, through a series of glands distributed in certain strategic areas of the body, discharges hormones directly into the bloodstream. Each endocrine hormone performs a different function and, in the case of migrating birds, at least one of the hormones serves to make the bird's body store fat for the long migration flight. Other hormones begin to stimulate the urge to breed and become restless, irritable with each other; and then, up they go into the sky, heading north or south according to the season. But do not yet accept this as fact, for it is but a theory, an educated one, it is true, but still requiring a great deal of confirmation. And there is also some evidence that birds can sense weather changes and these cause them to alter their migration times and perhaps their routes when they are warned by their internal 'barometers.'

For many centuries man has puzzled over the mysteries of bird migration and though today we have a few answers and have made some better guesses, still modern man has a long way to go before he can be expected to solve all the intricacies of the birds. And this is only just one more lesson in humility for us and one that is worth remembering when we feel that we have solved all the problems of life and pat ourselves smugly on the back. We have a very great deal to learn yet and nature, if we let her, is still our best teacher. At one time, undoubtedly like many others of my fellows, I believed that nature was a senseless collection of things chaotic, of jumbled up accidents that led to life which had no particular

purpose. Today I know that only in nature can we find true order and true freedom and dignity. Not that I am condemning man and his civilization, on the contrary! Man emerged from the order of nature, advanced through it and became the master. Now he has reached the most crucial stage of his orbit. Now he may continue to go on upwards; or he may stop rising, hesitate, and fall. I believe that man may yet learn wisdom from the wilderness, that he may yet have time to prevent his orbital plunge into atomic oblivion. But to derive value from nature, man must get to know her and, above all, he must learn to respect her; then he will find wisdom in what Alexander Graham Bell once said: "Don't keep forever on the public road. Leave the beaten track occasionally and dive into the woods. You will be certain to find something that you have never seen before, and before you know it you will have something worth thinking about to occupy your mind. All really big discoveries are the result of thought."

It was this kind of behaviour that led me, years ago, to an interesting discovery. I had often seen woodcock in the area of my property and I had almost as often remarked to myself at the strange position of this bird's eyes, which are enormous and placed high up and towards the back of its head. Where, I asked myself repeatedly, does this bird keep its brain? I looked up a number of reference books on the woodcock, but none of them mentioned its brain; then, one autumn, I found a dead woodcock. Somebody had shot it and wounded it and it had died in my woods. I dissected the bird's head and discovered that its brain, to my astonishment was positioned beneath its eyes. But after my surprise had worn off and I began to think about it, I found the woodcock's brain arrangement to be a most logical thing.

This squat, brownish relative of the sandpiper feeds almost exclusively on earthworms, thrusting its long, flexible beak into the ground and feeling for its prey. Now, any creature that spends so much of its time with its head so close to the ground must be in mortal danger in the wilderness, for there are many predators forever seeking an easy meal. So, in the fullness of time, nature

The woodcock is unique in that its eyes are placed towards the back of its head and its brain located beneath the eyes.

equipped the woodcock with eyes that can see when its head is almost buried in forest soil. But having given it these eyes, nature had to find a new place for its brain, because the vision mechanism now occupied the space where the brain should have been. And so the woodcock today enjoys a unique distinction, it has an upside-down brain.

In similar manner I made a few discoveries about skunks in general and one skunk in particular. In my forest country I am often the recipient of stray wild creatures found by my neighbours during early summer. Perhaps the wildling may be a bird, or a groundhog or a raccoon…or a skunk, as was more the case.

Young Billy Travis, a farm neighbour of mine, discovered the small, half starved skunk in a farmyard and, being a country boy,

he had no hesitation in capturing it. That was on a Friday morning and he and his parents came to me with the orphan. Now, most people are mortally afraid of skunks, be they large or small, and I must confess that when Sunday came and it was necessary to pack our baby stinker in our car, I had a few trepidations, for the little creature was well equipped with scent glands, and small though he was, one good spray in the car would have made life quite miserable on the return journey to the city. To complicate matters our Alaskan malamute dog, Tundra, who was then eleven weeks old, ignored tradition and persisted in making up to the skunk, who, strangely enough, appeared equally interested in the dog.

The first warning of this unnatural friendship came when Tundra lifted up on his great paws and padded back towards the end of my station wagon and lowered his nose to the skunk's cage. I held my breath. But nothing offensive happened. Instead the skunk waddled up to the wire and poked his nose through and the two sniffed each other placidly for a few moments. Because this was too much of a strain we managed to coax Tundra away and the remainder of the journey passed uneventfully, despite the bouncing and clatter to which the skunk was subjected.

Back in the city, the little stinker was housed in our garage. By this time he allowed me to scratch his head and was docile when I placed him on my lap and applied liberal quantities of flea powder and, if we took care to move slowly in his presence, he never once threatened us with a discharge of his guns. Slowly, I began to realize that this baby skunk was assessing his present situation as carefully as any human could have done. He learned the smell of my hand and very quickly associated it with food; he knew the dog and obviously realized that he was safe from it, protected by the bars of his cage, and even when Tundra became occasionally playful and bowed wolf-fashion and yapped loudly at him, the skunk did no more than lift his tail in half-warning and stamp his front feet. After that, if the dog persisted, he would simply turn his back on him and waddle sedately into the darkness of his nesting box. Now and then, if I forgot myself and moved too quickly for his

liking, the skunk would also warn me, but never once did he discharge his scent deliberately. And yet, on occasion, Joan or I would be made aware that we were housing a wild skunk which had not had its scent glands removed, and I often puzzled over this, for the strong musky aroma always seemed to materialize when the skunk was alone and, presumably, not alarmed. Then I happened to be squatting by his cage one day when he moved his bowels and I was given the answer to this puzzle. The poor little brute was a trifle constipated and the effort of passing his waste created undue pressure on his musk glands and some of the musk seeped out.

Like so many other discoveries that I have been making during the last six years or so, the peculiarities of the skunk and the woodcock are undoubtedly known to other naturalists, but each new discovery gives me a particular pleasure and shows me how little I really know about the wilderness. Thus, the animals and birds and insects, and even the trees and the plants, are my constant teachers and from them I obtain a steadily-increasing flow of values and I find more and more purpose in my life.

SEPTEMBER is my month. I was born on its twelfth day and have always looked to it with varying feelings; when I was a child the pleasures of parties of gifts were always mine in September; as a young man my Septembers seemed to come to me too slowly, sailing along in tempo with my downy beard, refusing to be hurried. And then came manhood and I caught up with my birth month, which now came quite quickly each year and, for a time, slipped by me nearly unnoticed, for my beard, once the symbol of a puberty period that I wished to hide, had grown bristly and was a nuisance and was sprinkled with the first threads of white. And now September comes along quietly for me. I still feel a faint stirring of childhood memories and I still look forward with young pleasure to the gift that Joan selects for me, but I neither want to hurry nor delay its arrival. Yet, it remains my month and, if each time that it comes it robs me of another year, it always gives me 365 days of memories and values as consolation, and it always

promises another twelve months of adventure in my wilderness. And at time like this, when I am beside my lake and I watch the slow fading of the water lilies, I look forward more keenly than ever to another unfolding of one more year in my life. Now I treasure the memories of those early Septembers and I regret the misuse of those Septembers that came in between puberty and manhood. Thus I resolve, each new September by my lake, to make full use of the years that lie ahead; and then, quite suddenly, September is gone. I have opened Joan's gifts and read my cards, I have eaten pieces of traditional cake, I have thought a bit on my youth, I have wondered at my future. But above all I have enjoyed my month in my wilderness, watching it unfurl itself pleasantly, crisp and golden; noticing its effects upon the forest and upon the water and in the air and upon the beasts and birds and insects of my forest world.

ON ONE OF THE WALLS of my cabin, Mrs. Little's calendar, the one that advertises her local store in the village of Uphill, has thinned down and its few remaining pages are dog-eared and fly-specked. It tells me that October has come. It reminds me that soon the birds will fly south, that the frosts will become more intense and that the snow will fly again shortly. Now and then I look at this calendar, a humble token of appreciation from a grand little lady, and I check the hours of daylight that are left to me during the tenth month. I regret the shortening of the days, yet I now begin to look forward to the coming of winter and to the flyless freedom of my wilderness. And, early though it may be, I climb into the cabin's loft and bring down my snowshoes, already anxious to strap them on to my moccasins and to be off on them, plodding for miles through the forest accompanied by my great wolf-dog Tundra. But I must have patience, for two full months lie between me and my winter freedom.

OCTOBER, and the lake shows each morning a thin skin of ice. The beaver are busy again, gnawing at poplar, felling and cutting and towing and 'planting' their supplies of winter food in the mud of lake bottom. Now the yellow tubers of the water lilies begin to float towards the banks, showing on their potato-like surfaces the chew marks of the teeth of the beaver, who have dug them up from the bottom and fed from them. The busbies of the catkins are fluffed and ragged and the muskrats are chopping down more and more of their stems. Some of my bird have already left me, others are congregating for their migration flight; the ducks are active on the lake, the geese have not yet returned from their northern breeding grounds. At night the timber wolf whelps try out their lungs and fill the forest with the haunting melodies of their songs; the whip-poor-wills sing more often, the bears show fat and sleek with summer fat, the buck deer are beginning to feel the madness of the rut.

Occasionally, cold rain slants down to pockmark the lake water, and on such days the sadness of the spent lily leaves and the fading of the waxen blooms seems accented by the rain. Small minnows scurry hungrily through the shallows, intent on garnering their food, falling prey to raccoons and turtles and bigger fish

The cheeky little chipmunk, busy preparing for the winter months.

and to the terns and gulls that now fly low over the water. The porcupines are browsing less on the ground and their round, black bodies are seen more often in the crowns of pine or poplar. And the leaves are beginning to fall; and the maples are dancing in scarlet and the poplars have bleached pale yellow and the oaks are russet; and the stiff little winds come more often and at each coming they pluck a few more colourful leaves from their bedding places on the tree branches.

On one such October I had launched my canoe and paddled to the island where the beaver have built their lodge. I sat in the craft, one hand holding to a scrub willow to keep the canoe from drifting, and I soaked up the atmosphere of my lake. I had been busy watching the water and the shores, spotting this bird or that, now and then catching sight of air bubbles drifting upwards from the depths as beaver or muskrat passed unseen beneath me. Perhaps half an hour I had remained thus, idle, watchful, when a reddish movement attracted my eyes to the west shore.

It was late afternoon and it had been a day of pleasant Indian Summer warmth. I had come here more for the peace of the place than in expectation of observing any of the dramas of the wilderness. But on this early evening I was to be a privileged spectator to a rare sight, for as I scanned with my glasses the area of the shoreline where the chestnut flash had signalled action, I uncovered the stealthy outline of a hunting fox, a magnificent dog, judging from his size and the slight mane around his neck and chest. He was nearly sliding along the ground in sinuous, patient stalk and I wondered what had captured his attention. I scanned the area ahead of him and soon discovered his prey. Sunning himself on an old pine stump was a groundhog, fat and sleek from fine summer living, made slothful by comfort as he let the late sun drench his roly-poly body.

The fox, glowing deep chestnut from where I watched, was about fifty yards away from his intended prey. The groundhog seemed oblivious, yet I knew that these creatures are amongst the most wary of the forest. The red fox was going to have to be extremely cunning and stealthy if he was to kill that woodchuck, I

said to myself, for the rodent, despite his sleepy appearance, had keen ears and a keen nose, even if his eyes were seemingly closed.

The groundhog remained immobile. The fox continued his slow advance. It was a marvellous thing to see how he took advantage of every bit of cover along his way! In places of scant cover he would flatten his body to the ground and crawl, inch by inch, never once showing signs of impatience. Where there was tall grass, he slid through the stems with hardly a shake of their tops and at such times he became invisible to me. In areas of brush he moved more quickly, keeping low and zig-zagging to take full advantage of his cover. Yard by yard he crept closer to his intended victim, who dozed on, oblivious of the death that was advancing inexorably towards him. I felt the excitement of this primitive drama. Here was life and death, twin companions of the wilderness, about to meet momentarily and then pass on. Civilization fled before me; it was though nothing else in the universe now existed except that fox and the groundhog. Which would win?

I am not sadistic and I do not watch such contests for the 'fun' of the thing. But I am inherently curious and analytical; I am also a believer in the laws of the wilderness and I tell you this because I feel that many of you, had you been in my place that evening, would have intervened on behalf of the groundhog; perhaps you would have shouted, or clapped your hands in warning. And if you had done either of these things you would have been wrong, for as surely as the sun sets and the moon comes to take its place, the fox must kill and the groundhog must die. The man who would interfere with the balance of the wilderness is neither helping the things and creatures of the forest, nor is he helping himself to understand the ways of the wild. So I sat and watched the drama that was unfolding before me and, although I had it in me to pity the groundhog, I also had it in me to pity the fox, for I, too, had been hungry in the past. For the most compelling law of all, even for the most civilized man amongst us, is the urge to satisfy the cravings of a shrunken, empty belly. Hunger is the call of life and all of us must respond to it, or perish.

After fifteen minutes of stalking, the fox had cut the distance to the groundhog by some twenty-five yards. Now the going was harder, for he was facing an area of open rock which, if he was to cross it, must surely alert the groundhog. So the fox stopped and studied the terrain. And he reasoned, and he retraced his careful steps a little way and detoured, slipping quietly into a place of dense marsh grass that hid him from my glasses and almost as certainly hid him from the groundhog. But now the hunter had doubled the distance of his stalk. To get around the rock flat and come up within striking reach of the groundhog, he would have to travel twice the distance that he had already come. Would he continue the hunt? He would. And did. Presently I saw him emerge from the grass and now he was below the groundhog, hidden from him. I could see his intention. He was aiming for a rise of land that was situated behind and above the intended victim. If he could reach this place unnoticed, the kill would be made. Only some two yards of downhill travel would separate him from the groundhog, which, close though it was to one of its burrows, would have little chance of evading the flashing teeth of the hunter. Half an hour elapsed during which time the fox was as often out of my view as he was in it. The groundhog continued, unaware of his nemesis. And then, fifty minutes after I had first seen the fox, he was positioned above his victim and pulling his lean body into the striking crouch. I held my breath. I counted silently. One, two, three, four…The fox propelled himself into space, landed and coiled himself into a flashing leap.

In the same instant that the fox sprang, the groundhog uttered a terrified whistle and uncoiled his fatness from the stump. For an instant it was anybody's game. Then the fox closed. I saw the gleaming canines fasten at the back of the groundhog's neck. There was a rolling flurry as they crashed bodies, then the fox regained his feet and the frantically threshing body of the seven or eight-pound rodent stilled as the fox jerked his neck sideways in the death twist. Back went the body of the groundhog, travelling with such force that it struck the fox high on the shoulder; but the

rodent's neck was imprisoned by the fox's teeth and the victim's own body, with its weight and momentum, snapped the creature's vertebrae. The groundhog was dead. Now it dangled limply from the fox's mouth, its hindquarters trailing in the red earth outside of its burrow. The fox lifted his head high and trotted away with his prize, now and then dragging the hindquarters along the trail, for the victim's weight was no small load for the killer. I watched as life and death disappeared into the shadows of the forest.

Recalling that wilderness drama, I am reminded that it was during that October that the young raccoon became trapped in the barrel in which Joan burns the combustible rubbish left over from our weekends on our property. We had arrived, as usual, on Friday night and we had noted that absence of the young raccoon, an adopted orphan given to us to look after by some city acquaintances who had been its first foster parents. We wondered what had happened to him. Perhaps he had fallen victim to a great horned owl, or to a wolf, or to a car. Though neither one of us voiced these feelings, each knew that the other was concerned, for the wilderness has drawn us more than usually closer to each other, and there are many occasions during which we do not require speech to become aware of each other's sentiments. That Friday night we slept away our concern and, with daylight and the coming of our many wild friends, thoughts of the little coon were edged back as we told ourselves that he would probably turn up again that night.

Then Joan went to deposit some garbage into the upright barrel. And next I heard her frantic call. By the time I reached her, she was returning with a little raccoon cradled in her arms and he was a sorry sight indeed. His pads were raw from his frantic efforts to escape from the imprisoning barrel, his fur was dull and grimed with cinders and iron dust, he was starving and terrified, and he clung to Joan for comfort and protection. Between us we cleaned him up and washed his bleeding pads and gave him a little water to drink and a little food to eat, but not too much, for an excess of either could have killed him. How long had he been in the barrel?

We do not know, but at least twenty-four hours, and probably more. He had evidently scaled the smooth walls of metal and then pitched head-first into the bottom, which, unluckily for him, Joan had all but cleaned out the Sunday before. Once in he could not escape.

For a time he slept in a box in the cabin, but all too soon, it seemed to us, he awoke and insisted on decamping into the woods. We followed his limping little figure as it moved along in clumsy imitation of a healthy raccoon's sinuous, rolling walk. He led us up on to a rock flat near our cabin and down again towards a ravine, and we watched as he went to ground into an empty groundhog burrow. For several weekends after that Joan would put titbits and peanuts down the hole, but we did not see him again that year and wondered if he was alive, or if he had gone down into that damp, quiet place to die.

Then came November. The last of the birds took wing and the great, waving Vs of Canada geese became once more silhouetted against the greying skies. Their calls echoed throughout the wilderness. We watched them, sad at their departure, for now we knew the autumn was almost done, and that the drab time of new winter was ahead of us and that many of our animals would leave us for another season.

The rains came cold, sleet mixed with them. The ice grew stronger on the edges of the lake and in the small pools throughout our wilderness. Dawns were hoary with frost and the ears tingled first thing in the morning. The broad-leaved trees were almost naked, their colours faded to browns and light yellows, showing now only faint traces of their former glories. The wolves howled more and, listening to them within the darkness of our cabin, I felt again the nostalgia of autumn.

Now my days of free-roaming through the wilderness would be shorter, my nights longer. My habits would begin to change as I altered to the ways of a northern winter fast approaching. Thus, sadness comes to me each autumn for a short time, for this is the dying time and the grace and beauty of true winter has not yet

arrived, and the memories of fresh spring days have not yet faded, and the fragrance of leafy summer still lingers in the mind. And in the morning, awakening to a sky that promises rain or sleet or snow, I rise and walk to my lake, there to catch a few last glimpses of late-departing geese, to listen one more time to their shrill cries as they wing south. And then, suddenly, it is all over.

The snow comes, at times driven by shrieking, furious winds; at other times softly. And it nestles upon the ground or it is driven with violence into the cracks of tree bark and into the crevices of rock. And then all things are white. Even the evergreens are mantled by the snow and their boughs hang downwards, weighted by the ice crystals, made pregnant by them. And then, as the storm passes, one by one the pine branches shake themselves loose from the heavy snows and there are cascades of white powder that fall to the ground as the limb that has rid itself of its burden springs back to its normal position. And the birds that will defy the winters of Canada return and voice their pleasure at the new white which they must endure for five months. The jays and the chickadees, and the nuthatches and the whiskey jacks; and the woodpeckers seem to become more busy as they drum on rotting trees.

The squirrels have shed their summer coats and are sleek and shiny in their winter garb of warmth; the small red squirrels with their shrill, spiteful calls; the docile, big black squirrels, shining ebony in the sunlight. Now I have dismissed the sadness of autumn and I give myself to the magic of winter in the wilderness. Now I can seek my snowshoes and prowl again for miles in the far distance of the forest. Now I can appreciate again the comfort of heavy clothing and the warmth of my cabin on my return to it. Now there is a new beauty in my wilderness.

I STAND BESIDE the place where the water lilies grow and I gaze over the white expanse that not too long ago was moving water filled with a million forms of life. I see the tracks of a wolf punched into the white surface. I see the trail of deer by the beaver lodge; the tracks of squirrels are clear in several places; the broad imprints of

snowshoe hares punctuate the marks left by the animals of winter. I look at the sky. It is blue, filled with sun, but there is only small warmth in the air about me. Again the hairs within my nostrils freeze, again my ears tingle from the bite of frost. It is time to move on, to retrace my route to Joan and to my cabin, to leave, for a short time at least, my lake; this place of wondrous secrets, of gorgeous water flowers. This place of happiness.

Credits for Illustrations

All visuals were taken by the author and used with his permission with the exception of the following, which are used with the permission of the photographers listed:

Jon Boxall	Snapping turtle, p.134
	American toad, p.145
Toni Harting	By canoe, p.159
Gordon Ramey	Great Blue Heron and nest, p.106
J.D. Taylor	Mallard duck, p.171
	Wood duck, p.171
	Canada geese, p.176
	Ruffed grouse, p.195
	Woodcock, p.207
Front Cover:	Toni Harting
Frontispiece:	Telfer Wegg
Back Cover:	Toni Harting

Index

Books by R.D. Lawrence

Wildlife in Canada (1966)
The Place in the Forest (1967, 1998)
Where the Water Lilies Grow (1968, 1999)
The Poison Makers (1969)
Cry Wild (1970)
Maple Syrup (1971)
Wildlife in North America: Mammals (1974)
Wildlife in North America: Birds (1974)
Paddy (1977)
The North Runner (1979)
Secret Go the Wolves (1980)
The Study of Life (1980)
The Zoo That Never Was (1981)
Voyage of the Stella (1982)
The Ghost Walker (1983)
Canada's National Parks (1983)
In Praise of Wolves (1986)
Trans Canada Country (1986)
The Natural History of Canada (1988)
For the Love of Mike (1989)
The White Puma (1989)
Wolves (1990)
Trail of the Wolf (1993)
The Green Trees Beyond (1994)
Shark! (1994)
A Shriek in the Forest Night (1996)
The Silent Fliers (1997)
The Snowshoe Hare Syndrome (in progress)

About the Author

R.D. LAWRENCE, the son of an English father and a Spanish mother was born at sea, aboard a British passenger ship sailing in Spanish territorial waters. His early years in Spain and his Spanish Civil War and World War II experiences are well documented in his autobiography *The Green Years Beyond*.

Since taking up residence in Canada in 1954, Lawrence has concerned himself with the environment and with the study of wildlife and plants. His contribution to our understanding of nature through his long-term field studies and award-winning publications is significant and continues to receive international acclaim.

The author of twenty-eight books, R.D. Lawrence is published in twenty-six countries and in fifteen languages.